EU Pension Law

T0311191

EU Pension Law

Hans van Meerten

with contributions of
Ton van den Brink, Pascal Borsjé, Elmar Schmidt and Jorik van Zanden

Amsterdam University Press

The publication of this book is made possible by sponsorship from

STATE STREET GLOBAL ADVISORS

Cover design: Gijs Mathijs Ontwerpers
Lay-out: Crius Group, Hulshout

ISBN	978 94 6372 521 7
e-ISBN	978 90 4854 453 0
DOI	10.5117/9789463725217
NUR	825

Contents

Abbreviations   9

Preface   11

Foreword   15

1   Introduction   19
    1.1   The creation of an EU pensions union   19
    1.2   Aging and new risks   20
    1.3   The EU Treaty: Precedence over national law   22
    1.4   The three pension pillars   22
          1.4.1   The first pillar   24
          1.4.2   The second pillar   24
          1.4.3   The third pillar   25
          1.4.4   The different pension pillars of Europe   26

2   The impact of the EU's institutional system on pensions law   27
    2.1   Introduction   27
    2.2   EU competences to regulate pensions: The principle of
          conferred powers   27
    2.3   The exercise of EU competences: The principles of subsidiarity
          and proportionality   35
          2.3.1   Subsidiarity   35
          2.3.2   Proportionality   40
    2.4   Legislation and administrative rule-making   43
          2.4.1   Introduction   43
          2.4.2   Distinguishing legislative and non-legislative acts   44
          2.4.3   Delegation and implementation   48
    2.5   Rule-making and EU agencies   53

3   Occupational pensions and the freedom to provide services   55
    3.1   Introduction   55
    3.2   Compulsory membership and the freedom to provide services   57
          3.2.1   Compulsory membership: An obstacle to the freedom
                  to provide services?   58
          3.2.2   Justifying obstacles to the freedom to provide services   59
          3.2.3   The UNIS case   64

3.3 Comparison: Mandatory participation in a selection of
    Member States   65
    3.3.1   Compulsory membership in the Netherlands   65
         3.3.1.1   The Bpf Act and the Wvb   66
         3.3.1.2   Compulsory membership in the Netherlands:
                    Direct discrimination   67
    3.3.2   Sweden   68
    3.3.3   Denmark   69
    3.3.4   Germany   70
    3.3.5   Belgium   72
    3.3.6   France   73
3.4 Concluding remarks   75

4   **The Institution for Occupational Retirement Provision**
    (IORP) Directive   77
4.1 Introduction   77
4.2 Scope of the directive   79
4.3 General observations on the IORP Directive   82
    4.3.1   Background to IORP Directive revision: On IORPs and
          insurers   83
4.4 Revision of the IORP Directive: IORP II   86
    4.4.1   Legal basis   86
    4.4.2   Cross-border activity and applicable requirements   88
         4.4.2.1   Funding requirements and cross-border
                    schemes   88
         4.4.2.2   Scope of cross-border regulations under IORP II 92
    4.4.3   The prudent person principle and investment rules   94
    4.4.4   System of governance and risk-management requirements 95
         4.4.4.1   System of governance   95
         4.4.4.2   Risk-management requirements   97
    4.4.5   Information requirements and supervisory instruments   99
         4.4.5.1   Pensions and fundamental European rights   100
         4.4.5.2   Guarantees   101
         4.4.5.3   Funding requirements   103
         4.4.5.4   Information requirements and supervision
                    under the IORP II Directive   105
4.5 Freedom of movement safeguarded?   108
4.6 Tax aspects   109
4.7 Final observations   111

5   Application of EU law on pensions: The property issue   113
    5.1   Introduction   113
    5.2   Article 17 Charter and Article 1 FP ECHR   113
          5.2.1   Different wording   115
          5.2.2   ECJ case law   116
                  5.2.2.1   The *Hogan* case   118
                  5.2.2.2   The *Hampshire* case   121
    5.3   Direct horizontal effect: The ECHR v Charter   121
    5.4   Application of the Charter to pension institutions   123
    5.5   Conclusion   125

6   PEPP   127
    6.1   Introduction   127
    6.2   The pan-European personal pension product (PEPP)   128
          6.2.1   Legal basis   128
                  6.2.1.1   The freedom to provide services and the
                            compartment approach   129
          6.2.2   The PEPP as a framework   130
          6.2.3   The authorization of a PEPP   132
          6.2.4   Eligible providers   134
          6.2.5   Distribution and information requirements   135
          6.2.6   The default and alternative investment options   136
          6.2.7   Investment rules   138
          6.2.8   Out-payments   139
    6.3   Conclusion   140

Index   141

Abbreviations

AG	advocate general
AOW	General Old Age Pensions Act (*Algemene Ouderdomswet*) of the Netherlands
Apf	general pension fund (*algemeen pensioenfonds*) of the Netherlands
BEPG	broad economic policy guidelines
BetrAVG	Betriebsrentengesetz (Company Pensions Act) of Germany
Bpf	sectoral pension fund (*bedrijfstakpensioenfonds*) of the Netherlands
Bpf Act	Act on Compulsory Membership of a Sectoral Pension Fund 2000
CFR	Charter of Fundamental Rights of the European Union
CMU	capital markets union
CRD	Capital Requirements Directive
CSR	country-specific recommendation
DB	defined benefit
DC	defined contribution
EC	European Commission
ECJ	European Court of Justice
ECtHR	European Court of Human Rights
EEA	European Economic Area
EIOPA	European Insurance and Occupational Pensions Authority
EMPL	Committee on Employment and Social Affairs of the European Parliament
EMU	Economic and Monetary Union
EP	European Parliament
ESA	European supervisory authority
ESG	environmental, social and governance
ESMA	European Securities and Markets Authority
EU	European Union
FP	first protocol
GDP	gross domestic product
IA	impact assessment
IDD	Insurance Distribution Directive
IIA	Interinstitutional Agreement between the European Parliament, the Council of the European Union and the European Commission on Better Law-Making
IORP	institution for occupational retirement provision
KID	key information document
MiFID	Markets in Financial Instruments Directive
OECD	Organisation for Economic Co-operation and Development
OMC	open method of coordination
ORSA	own risk and solvency assessment

PAYG	pay-as-you-go
PEPP	pan-European personal pension product
PPI	premium pension institution
PRIIP	packaged retail and insurance-based investment product
QIS	Quantitative Impact Study
TEU	Treaty on the European Union
TFEU	Treaty on the Functioning of the European Union
UCITS	Undertakings for Collective Investment in Transferable Securities
Wvb	Wet verplichte beroepspensioenregeling (Mandatory Professional Pension Scheme Act) of the Netherlands

Preface

EU pension law – a unique field

Among scores of publications on the topic of pensions, there are remarkably few that focus on European pension law. Their focus is mostly local, often on domestic pension solutions and not on cross-border innovations. There is often reluctance to delve deeper into useful pension experiences from abroad as well. This book is different.

EU pension law is a relatively new and rapidly growing field. The call for knowledge of EU pension law and a broader practical understanding is growing, as pension markets are increasingly internationalized. More experts in this field are desperately needed.

This handbook contains a collection of relevant articles and offers necessary basic knowledge. More importantly, it contains interesting practical cases, creating a unique bridge between theory and practice. Whether you are a student, a committed policymaker, an experienced market practitioner, or 'just' someone interested in European pension developments, this handbook is designed for you.

European pension solutions in practice

The growing need for EU pension law knowledge is most striking in two areas. On the one hand, the effects of EU law are becoming increasingly prevalent on local pension markets, while on the other, it remains important in the European internal pension market.

In the local Member States, awareness about the influence of EU law is often limited. Pension provisions are based on local social, labour and tax law. This domain largely belongs to the mandate of the Member States and therefore falls outside the EU sphere of influence. It is often insufficiently recognized and acknowledged that EU pension law determines pension systems in Member States through other means. After all, Member States must comply with EU legislation and implement it in local legislation. In addition, we increasingly experience in legal practice how European law overrules local law.

This concerns, for example, the governance structure of pension institutions and competition legislation, property law and tax non-discrimination legislation, but also EU legislation on new pension products, investment and communication policy. The European Pensions Directive, which regulates pension institutions, is a good example of the enormous impact of EU law on local pension markets.

In the cross-border European pension market on the contrary, awareness about the influence of EU pension law has traditionally been very high. EU legislation provides the foundation for being able to act freely in the EU internal market, as a working and pension participant, as an employer and plan sponsor, and as a pension provider and service provider. It is elementary to its function. The EU internal market for capital, labour, and services is growing. Cross-border activities and solutions are by definition based on EU pension law.

For example, multinational companies have established cross-border pension funds (cross-border institutions for occupational retirement provision or IORPs), which manage pension schemes for participants from different countries. This is a steadily growing market segment. The PEPP (pan-European personal pension product) has also been created for cross-border use. The PEPP encourages retirement savings in Member States where this still receives little attention, and serves the growing group of internationally mobile workers. Increased standardization allows more providers to be active across borders, increases the quality of the products and lowers fees.

Both the IORP and the PEPP are pension solutions initiated by the EU with the aim to meet new needs in the market and to support the European capital market and make long-term funding sources available.

International collaboration

As part of the EU internal market, Member States increasingly exchange pension knowledge and experience. Local pension systems are different. However, the underlying trends are the same and require similar legislative changes and modern, innovative solutions.

These trends include having to work longer as we all get older, the need to combine part-time retirement and continued work, and the need for more insight and making pension saving easier through finance technology solutions, such as apps and robo-advice. Countries can learn from each other how pension provisions can be personalized, with more options and tailor-made solutions. The 'gig economy' has a strong need for this flexibility to enable increased financial health in old age.

EU pension forums allow for this cooperation across borders, for example, through the European Commission, the European Parliament and the European pension authority, EIOPA. The various interest groups in the pension sector, such as PensionsEurope, the European Fund and Asset Management Association (EFAMA) and the Cross Border Benefits Alliance (CCBA), also support the exchange of best practices. All of these bodies need experts who are trained in EU pension law.

State Street Global Advisors

State Street Global Advisors wholeheartedly supports the creation of this European pension law handbook. We are an international pension asset manager and service provider and have been at the core of the pension sector for many years and in many countries. We not only help ensure that people receive good pension benefits, but also facilitate efficient retirement saving for working people, by providing them with an understanding of and control over their pension plan, thereby giving them the confidence and peace of mind that they are well on track on their 'pension journey'. We ensure a sound investment policy with a controlled degree of risk-taking and provide asset management administration and accessible reporting. Our strength is innovation through the exchange of experience and knowledge across borders and regions.

Sometimes our company name is prominent, as in this handbook. More often we work behind the scenes, where our asset management services, pension solutions and thought leadership help pension funds and policymakers.

In conclusion

The more experts there are to help shape the above-mentioned European pension developments, the better. These experts should have a deep understanding of European law and acknowledge its importance. These experts should by nature have an international perspective and look beyond national borders, and stimulate exchange of knowledge and experience between countries.

Prof. Dr Hans van Meerten has taken the lead. He is an initiator in the field of European pension law, a scholar who knows how to combine his knowledge, experience and network with his scientific role as a professor at the University of Utrecht. He is also a researcher, who does not hesitate to actively propagate and safeguard European ideas in local pension sectors. We are proud to support him in this endeavour.

Marie-Anne Heeren
Head of Continental Europe
State Street Global Advisors

Foreword

Before you lies the book *EU Pension Law*. This is a new field of law and it foresees in a growing need for universities and practice throughout the EU.

Pension law is approached mainly from a national point of view. An EU point of view is lacking. The book tries to shed some light on a number of important pension issues that should be approached from an EU perspective.

It discusses the most important financial EU legislation (IORP and PEPP) and non-financial legislation (such as the Charter of Fundamental Rights of the European Union [CFR]) and how it has consequences for pensions.

EU Pension Law comprises a plethora of legal fields, such as financial law, company law, competition law, etc.

We therefore needed to make a selection. This book deals with the following – we believe the most important – issues:

- The EU competences in the field of pensions
- The IORP I and II Directives
- Compulsory membership in an IORP
- Application of EU law on pensions: The property issue
- The PEPP

The EU competences in the field of pensions

Pension is often perceived as a national competence. This chapter sets out the fact that numerous EU laws give the EU competence to regulate national pension systems.

The central question in this chapter is how the institutional system of the EU affects the regulation of pensions at the EU level. First, the powers of the EU to regulate pensions and the way in which these are defined and limited will be examined. This involves the principles of conferred powers, subsidiarity and proportionality which establish and regulate the exercise of EU legislative powers. The second part of this chapter addresses the EU legislative system with its distinction between legislative, delegated and implementing acts. Each of these acts has individual characteristics, defining the specific powers and roles of the EU institutions and the matter such acts may cover. The impact thereof on EU pensions legislation will be assessed.

The IORP I and II Directives

In 2003, the European legislature issued a directive on the activities and supervision of institutions for occupational retirement provision (IORPs). The IORP Directive as adopted in 2003 sets a number of general solvency and financing requirements, certain investment rules (based on the prudent person principle) and general administrative and governance requirements (in particular regarding the provision of information. The IORP Directive of 2003 ('IORP I Directive' or 'IORPD I') has been subject to revision, and the recast directive ('IORP II Directive' or 'IORPD II') was published in 2016 and came into force in January 2017.

This chapter describes the IORP I and II Directives and its cross-border legal framework.

Compulsory membership in an IORP

This chapter explains, first, the relationship between compulsory membership and European law and jurisprudence from the European Court of Justice (ECJ or the Court). It will then study how compulsory membership is organized in the Netherlands and a selection of other EU countries and will assess those systems of (quasi-) mandatory participation from the perspective of European law and the ECJ's case law. Because of the size of the Dutch schemes, some extra attention will be paid to the Netherlands.

The main question that is addressed in this chapter is: Can a justification be found in EU law for mandatory participation in a pension fund and/or in a pension scheme?

Application of EU law on pensions: The property issue

Since the entry into force of the Charter of Fundamental Rights of the European Union ('the Charter') in 2009, it can be argued that all of the European Union's general principles of law are essentially 'covered.' The Charter codifies, directly or indirectly, all existing EU fundamental rights and legal principles. According to Barents and Brinkhorst, it can even be stated that the Charter must always be applied by the ECJ as well as the national courts.[1]

In this Chapter we want to address the property rights issue, a fundamental right both covered by the Charter and the European Convention on Human Rights (ECHR). How are your pension rights protected?

---

1   R. Barents, L.J. Brinkhorst, *Grondlijnen van Europees Recht* (Deventer: Kluwer, 2012).

The PEPP

On 29 June 2017, the European Commission proposed a framework for a pan-European personal pension product (PEPP).

This framework aims to offer EU citizens a value for money option to acquire an income after retirement. Furthermore, the PEPP could help in meeting the objectives of the capital markets union (CMU) by increasing voluntary pension savings, aiding savers by expanding the available market of personal pension products and enabling providers to offer products to a larger customer base.

The pan-European personal pension product is a one of a kind initiative by the Commission to strengthen the CMU. While most European legislation governing pensions is aimed at establishing prudential requirements for pension providers, the PEPP creates a 'label', guaranteeing the quality of certain features of the product itself. One of the key features of the PEPP is that it is a portable product, in which savers can continue to contribute after moving from one Member State to another. However, considering that only 3.7% of the working population of the EU is considered a mobile worker, the added value of the PEPP may be especially prevalent in Member States without well-developed multi-pillar pension systems.

The chapters in this book are the result of new insights and include sections that are prepared on the basis of existing articles which I partly co-wrote with different authors. These are Ton van den Brink, Pascal Borsjé, Elmar Schmidt and Jorik van Zanden.

May 2019

1   Introduction[1]

'[N]ormal' services and financial services differ in a number of ways.
This can result in linguistic confusion. A 'classic EU lawyer' involved in
financial EU law would be wise to bear this in mind.[2]

1.1   The creation of an EU pensions union

Over the recent years, a wide variety of policy areas has been becoming
increasingly internationalized, including the area of old age pensions. Social
security, on the other hand, the area to which pensions in a large number
of countries belong, seems to insist on remaining a national matter. A
statement heard in many circles is that 'Europe should not interfere with
our pensions.' This is usually followed by: 'We can manage very well on our
own, thank you; we don't need Europe for that.'

The majority of the political representatives and many pension funds seem
to share this attitude. The question arises whether it is really possible – or,
for a number of reasons – desirable to exclude the European Union when
designing a national pension system. Is it really true that 'Europe' should
'keep its nose out' of 'our' pension systems? As is often the case, matters are
not as black and white as they may seem, and a different perspective could
cast new light on the subject.

The Member States of the European Union (EU) not only can, but really
must conclude that the influence of the EU on national pension systems is
very necessary. Take as an example the problem of setting the pension age
in a given country: is it not strange that in one country this can be set at 55,
and in another EU country at 67? This disparity is particularly troublesome
given that in many countries, including those with a lower pension age,
a large part of the population is rapidly reaching the age of retirement.[3]

---

1   Parts of this chapter appeared earlier in: H. Van Meerten, J.J. van Zanden, 'Pensions and the
PEPP: The Necessity of an EU Approach', *European Company Law Journal* 15.3 (2018).

2   H. van Meerten, 'De premiepensioeninstelling: van, maar ook op alle markten thuis?',
Nederlands tijdschrift voor Europees recht 12 (2008).

3   'The demographic old-age dependency ratio set to nearly double over the long-term', according
to the European Commission in *The 2015 Ageing Report*: http://ec.europa.eu/economy_finance/
publications/european_economy/2015/pdf/ee3_en.pdf. Then Dutch minister of economic affairs,
Laurens Jan Brinkhorst, already warned about this in 2004: http://www.nu.nl/financieel/284952/
pensioenleeftijd-te-laag.html.

Furthermore, many EU countries share the same currency, interlinking the sustainability of their economies in which pension expenditure is a large part of the GDP.[4]

A call for greater European cooperation in the area of pensions is unpopular among a number of players in the pension sector. Greater EU cooperation appears, however, to be in the interest of pension participants.

We should not forget the reason for having a pension scheme in the first place: to provide participants greater protection in their old age. This protection comes predominantly from Brussels and is also enshrined in the Charter of Fundamental Rights of the EU.[5]

Meanwhile more and more people are seeing that solely national organization of pension systems has at least a number of significant deficiencies.

1.2   Aging and new risks

The increasingly ageing European populations have been a concern of national governments in relation to pensions. For many years, the number of pension beneficiaries is increasing at a higher rate than the economically active population required to fund the pension benefits,[6] which puts severe pressure on the public finances and the affordability of pensions.[7] The projected old age dependency ratio (people from 65 and above relative to those aged 15-64) will amount to 50.1% in 2060, in comparison to 27.8% in 2014.[8]

At EU level, concerns about the future affordability of the pension systems and the flexibility of the labour market (with pensions being part of the internal market) have been the focus of much attention.

Besides the aging population, European citizens are becoming mobile, making use of their right to the freedom of movement for workers. In 2015, 3.7% of the European population was living in a Member State other than that of their citizenship, equating to 11.3 million people.[9] Current pension

---

4   The necessity of having a sustainable and well-developed pension system is part of the EU Stability and Growth Pact.

5   Article 25 (Charter of Fundamental Rights of the European Union [CFR]), see below.

6   Cf. European Commission, *Dealing with the Impact of an Ageing Population in the EU: 2009 Ageing Report* (2009).

7   European Parliamentary Research Service (EPRS), 'Demographic Outlook for the European Union' (2017).

8   Van Meerten and Van Zanden, 'Pensions and the PEPP'.

9   European Court of Auditors, 'Free Movement of Workers – The Fundamental Freedom Ensured but Better Targeting of EU Funds Would Aid Worker Mobility', Special report no. 06 (2018), https://www.eca.europa.eu/Lists/ECADocuments/SR18_06/SR_Labour_Mobility_EN.pdf.

systems cannot easily accommodate 'portability' between Member States. EU initiatives such as the IORP Directive, to be discussed in Chapter 4 of this book, do not seem to suffice to solve this problem.

As stated above, different actors deem full national competence paramount for the safeguarding of their pension systems. The 2008 and 2012 financial crises, however, prove the vulnerability of markets and display the vast amount of damage and hardship that may occur – especially – to the individual savers.

In that sense, pensions are a hybrid of social, labour and financial factors. In any event, they are not a stand-alone, but rather benefit or suffer at the whims of the financial market.

To safeguard consumers, the European Union has implemented several regulations and directives to cushion the blows of financial crises. For example, the CRD IV Directive, designed to protect banks against the heaviest financial crises in 200 years, the MiFID II and IDD Directives, designed to provide protection against unsafe financial instruments and for pensions specifically: the IORP II Directive.

The IORP Directive can be used as an illustration of the vast variety of pension landscapes within the EU and the political sensitivity of the topic. While the IORP Directive is aimed at safeguarding pensioners from losing their retirement income, it is still characterized by its approach of minimum harmonization in order to accommodate the myriad of national systems.

Pension law, including European pension law, consist of European financial and company law, to a significant extent.[10] As stated above, many financial institutions are currently active both within and outside of the EU, based on the UCITS,[11] Solvency II[12] and CRD IV Directives.[13] These are mostly abbreviations for investment firms, insurance companies and banking institutions that are regulated at the EU level. Technically, it can be argued that a European banking union exists already.

---

10   For example, the Dutch Commission of Insurers (Commissie Verzekeraars) is a proponent of a European 'Insurance union'. See Commissie Verzekeraars, 'Nieuw leven voor verzekeraars', 5 March 2015.

11   Council Directive 85/611/EEC (UCITS) has been significantly revised a number of times. In the fourth revision the directive was restructured: see Directive 2009/65/EG.

12   Directive 2009/138/EC on the taking-up and pursuit of the business of insurance and reinsurance (Solvency II) replaced the current insurance directive (Solvency I) and was to enter into force in 2016.

13   Originally: Directive 2006/48/EC relating to the taking up and pursuit of the business of credit institutions.

The idea behind this legislation is that it would be unfair to expect citizens to bear the costs of banking deficiencies or losses. This idea, a form of consumer protection, can be found behind other EU legislation as well. Why should something different apply to pension funds? Because pension funds are 'social institutions'?

This book tries to shed some light on these questions. First however, we want to address a few 'general EU law' issues.

1.3   The EU Treaty: Precedence over national law

In short, there exist the Treaty on the European Union (TEU) and the Treaty on the Functioning of the European Union (TFEU). Too little attention is paid to these important EU treaties in national pension discussions, despite the fact that we have known since 1963 that this treaty is supranational and has priority over national legislation.

The famous *Van Gend en Loos* case cannot go without reference. In that case the European Court of Justice held that European law constitutes its own autonomous legal order, with priority over conflicting national law.[14] Over the course of time a great number of European directives and regulations came about that are directly or indirectly applicable to 'our pensions' – in addition to the free movement provisions. In other words: Europe has been 'interfering' with our pensions for decades.

Of particular relevance to pensions is the free movement provision enshrined in Article 56 TFEU. Article 56 TFEU plays an important role in this discussion as it provides that services should be freely provided within the EU. The IORP Directive is based in part on this treaty provision.[15] According to the ECJ, the Pensions Directive aims to create an internal market for occupational pension provision in which the occupational pension providers must be free to perform services and investments throughout the territory of the EU.[16]

1.4   The three pension pillars

To understand the issues of pensions throughout Europe, a brief description of the pension layout will be provided.

---

14   C-26/62.
15   Besides Article 56 TFEU, the directive is based also on Articles 62 and 114(1) TFEU.
16   C-343/08, C-678/11.

Pensions are commonly (and roughly) divided into three pillars, all regulated by different principles and legislation. The first pillar is state sponsored, generally funded via a pay-as-you-go system, or covered directly from taxes. The first pillar is generally considered a pure social matter, and available in some Member States to individuals without prejudice to any history of employment. The second pillar is linked to the status of employment. Workers enrol in a collective pension scheme via their employers, either mandatorily or voluntarily. In some Member States, the second pillar pension makes up for the biggest part of the retirement income of the retiree. The third pillar consists of a pension savings plan that was purchased on an individual level. These are not linked to any employment status and governed by the principle of the market. It must be noted that these pillars are not strictly separated from each other, but act as a general divide between the different sources of retirement income. Some 'borderline' cases are imaginable, such as a group personal pension in which the social partners choose a pension, that the employer voluntarily offers.[17] On a European level, the European Insurance and Occupational Pensions Authority (EIOPA) leaves it to the Member States to determine if a pension is considered a second or third pillar product.[18]

However, the divide between second and third pillar products is relevant when considering the applicable legislation. For example: if an employer offers to contribute to a third pillar product on behalf of an employee, it may be argued that this third pillar product has become a second pillar product – at the very least, it has taken on characteristics of one.

Since the publication of *Averting the Old Age Crisis: Policies to Protect the Old and Promote Growth* by the World Bank in 1994,[19] the use of the three pillars to divide different pension schemes has become a well-known and broadly used concept.[20] These three pillars are often described as the public, occupational and voluntary individual pension pillar.[21] But this distinction does not stand alone, some differentiate in the objectives of the pillar, which are (1) insuring against old age poverty, (2) insuring against inadequate

17   J.J. van Zanden, 'Het PEPP: is er nog een pijler op te trekken?', *PensioenMagazine* 34 (2017).
18   EIOPA, 'Towards an EU Single Market for Personal Pensions: An EIOPA Preliminary Report to COM', EIOPA-BoS-14/029.
19   World Bank, *Averting the Old Age Crisis: Policies to Protect the Old and Promote Growth* (Washington, DC: World Bank, 1994).
20   Directorate-General for Internal Policies, 'Pension Schemes: Study for the EMPL Committee', PE 536.281.
21   R. Davies, 'Occupational Pensions: Second Pillar Provision in the EU Policy Context', European Parliament Library Briefing, European Parliament, Brussels, 2013.

replacement of income during retirement and (3) encouraging voluntary pension savings.[22]

The distinction between the pillars is often made using (1) the mechanism of funding and (2) the mandatory or individual participation of the fund.[23]

1.4.1   The first pillar

Even within this pillar the differences between the schemes are enormous. For example, between the different Member States of the EU the goals within the first pillars are not completely uniform. The OECD makes a distinction between three different sub-types of the first pillar. Firstly, a 'basic' first pillar pension scheme uses a flat rate of benefits, or benefits linked to labour market participation.[24] The Dutch state pension, the AOW (General Old Age Pensions Act) system, for example, is linked to the years of domicile within the Kingdom of the Netherlands. Every year of residence within the Netherlands grants the right of 2% of the total AOW benefit, which means that the full right to the Dutch first pillar pension is reached after 50 years of residence, not linked to any requirements of labour market participation.[25] Secondly, 'minimum' pension schemes have the goal of ensuring that a minimum of pension benefits is guaranteed. If the income from the other pillars is insufficient, the first pillar will contribute to the retirees' income, until the minimum is reached. Thirdly, targeted distribution may be used for specific individuals, taking into account their specific needs.

All three sub-versions of the first pillar may be used in the same system, which can feature both a targeted and a minimum system, like in Belgium or even all three, like in Luxembourg and Malta.[26]

1.4.2   The second pillar

The second pillar is aimed at an adequate replacement of income after retirement.[27] In a sense, this pillar is an insurance against the inability to be employed after retirement. The amount for which an employee is insured differs in both the different systems throughout the EU and the individual saver. The second pillar is linked to occupational schemes, which often have

---

22   OECD, *Pensions at a Glance: Public Policies across OECD, 2005* (Paris: OECD Publishing).
23   Directorate-General for Internal Policies, 'Pension Schemes'.
24   Ibid.
25   https://www.svb.nl/int/nl/aow/hoogte_aow/hoeveel_aow_later/.
26   Directorate-General for Internal Policies, 'Pension Schemes'.
27   Ibid.

a defined benefit (DB) or a defined contribution (DC) mechanism. The defined benefit schemes often have a redistribution element, depending on the design.[28] In the Netherlands, a norm of 70% of the medial income after retirement was thought to be the defined benefit. However, like the pay-as-you-go system, defined benefit systems are vulnerable to changing demographics and economic environments. In some countries, the defined benefit scheme is linked with a mandatory participation of the employee. In contrast to the first pillar pension schemes, this participation (mandatory or voluntary) is linked to privately managed pension schemes.

As mentioned before, a distinction within the second pillar may be made to (1) the use of defined benefit and (2) defined contribution schemes. In the latter, the investment risk is borne by the saver, while a defined benefit guarantees a certain amount in the pay-out phase, leaving any investment risks to be borne by the provider.[29] A defined benefit is closely linked to the actual participation in the labour market, while a defined contribution scheme has a closer link to the actual earnings.

1.4.3 The third pillar

The three main characteristics of the third pillar are pension schemes that are (1) private, (2) voluntary and (3) funded.[30] Most of these schemes are based on defined contribution, complementing the individual character of the third pillar. However, providers are not bound to offer DC schemes, so pensions in the third pillar may be quite diverse. This is also a reason why third pillar pension products may be nearly indistinguishable from some second pillar products.

These 'borderline cases' combine the voluntary nature of the third pillar with an element of employment.[31] Some of these are even sold as both occupational and personal, such as the British 'group personal pension'.[32] Furthermore, occupational pension schemes with an opt-out option can be considered voluntary, as well as closely linked to employment. Individual contractual agreements between an employer and employee in which the first pays a contribution to a pension scheme of the choosing of the latter are both voluntary and closely linked to the employment.

---

28 Ibid.
29 Directorate-General for Internal Policies, 'Pension Schemes'.
30 Ibid.
31 Van Zanden, 'Het PEPP'.
32 EIOPA, 'Towards an EU Single Market'.

1.4.4   The different pension pillars of Europe

As stated above, it is not always possible to create a clear distinction between the different products and pension pillars. While it is argued in The
Netherlands that a pension product/scheme is 'second pillar' as soon as any
form or involvement of employment is involved,[33] other jurisdictions have
completely voluntary individual second pillar schemes, such as Belgium,[34]
which The Netherlands might classify as 'third pillar'. As a consequence, in
cross-border situations uncertainty about applicable legislation may occur.[35]
This might be a problem when creating European legislation.

A 'pension' aims to offer a saver an income after retirement and/or a
certain age. This broad aim is governed by numerous sectors of law, such as
social, labour, financial and tax legislation. However, once the cross-border
element is added, an even wider scope of legislation becomes applicable,[36]
not in the last place the different freedoms under the EU Treaty and the
EU Charter of Fundamental Rights.

Most importantly, if a pension scheme can be qualified as 'occupational',
Article 45 TFEU in principle applies, granting the pension participant additional rights under the freedom of workers.

After all, if an EU citizen qualifies as a 'worker', Article 45 TFEU grants
him the right to work in another Member State than his home Member
State. The ECJ has ruled that under Article 45 TFEU workers must be able
to retain their pension rights when migrating.[37] Workers who have worked
in multiple Member States should not be disadvantaged in comparison with
those who have lived in the same Member State.[38]

These issues will be dealt in detail in the following chapters.

---

33   Van Zanden, 'Het PEPP'.
34   Such as *pensioenovereenkomst voor zelfstandigen* (POZ), pension schemes for the
self-employed.
35   H. van Meerten, B. Starink, 'Impediments to an Internal Market for Institutions for Occupational Retirement Provision', *European Company Law* 7.6 (2010).
36   Although in purely internal situations EU Law also applies. See: C-31/16.
37   C-379/09.
38   Idem.

2 The impact of the EU's institutional system on pensions law[1]

2.1 Introduction

The central question in this chapter is how the institutional system of the EU affects the regulation of pensions at the EU level. First, the powers of the EU to regulate pensions and the way in which these are defined and limited will be examined. This involves the principles of conferred powers, subsidiarity and proportionality which establish and regulate the exercise of EU legislative powers. The second part of this chapter addresses the EU legislative system with its distinction between legislative, delegated and implementing acts. Each of these acts has individual characteristics, defining the specific powers and roles of the EU institutions and the matter such acts may cover. The impact thereof on EU pensions legislation will be assessed.

2.2 EU competences to regulate pensions: The principle of conferred powers

Is the EU competent to regulate pensions? The question is key: pensions are often considered to belong to the national domain, and also in light of the lack of general EU legislative powers. The principle of conferred powers prescribes that the EU may only act if and when the Member States have explicitly attributed the EU with the power to do so.[2] The EU treaties, the Treaty on the EU (TEU) and the Treaty on the Functioning of the European Union (TFEU), in particular, are therefore the key documents to assess whether the EU may indeed regulate pensions in general or certain aspects thereof. These treaties include a long list of legal bases that create competences for the EU to regulate a myriad of policy areas. However, pensions law is no area in which the EU has such a specific legislative authority. Yet, this does not make the area immune to involvement of the

---

1   This chapter has been authored by Ton van den Brink. See also: A. van den Brink, H. van Meerten, 'EU Executive Rule-Making and the Second Directive on Institutions for Occupational Retirement Provision', *Utrecht Law Review* 12.1 (2016).
2   Article 4(1) TEU.

EU legislature. As will be discussed below, this may be explained by the way in which the EU system of division of competences has been elaborated and applied in practice.

The choice of legal basis for legislative acts is often a controversial issue in legislative decision-making. It may seem straightforward that every legislative act should be based on a competence from the treaties and that it should be clear which legal basis should be chosen. The reality is, however, that this choice is often far from unambiguous. At the same time, the ECJ has decided that the choice of legal basis 'may not only depend on an institution's conviction [...] but must be based on *objective factors* which are amenable to judicial review' (emphasis added). Thus, the choice of legal basis is not only in the hands of the EU's political institutions; ultimately the ECJ can decide on the legality of EU legislation in light of the chosen legal basis. Leino has demonstrated how the competence issue is indeed Janus-faced, combining the aspect of competence being an objective, judicially review-able matter and at the same time a matter of political choice. The result is not necessarily an attempt to bridge the unbridgeable. The formal rules function as (outer) limits and leave considerable discretion to the political institutions.[3] Political choices in their turn are often framed and argued in legal terminology.[4] The political and legal aspects of the competence issue are therefore more closely intertwined than one may expect.

The lack of a specific legal basis to regulate pensions is thus not the end of the story. From an EU perspective, pensions and pension systems directly impact the functioning of the EU's internal market, most notably the free movement of persons and services. In this field, the EU has ample competence to regulate. Commonly applied is Article 114 TFEU which creates the competence for the EU to adopt measures to harmonize national laws, regulations or administrative actions to establish or to improve the functioning the internal market. The scope of this provision is ex-tremely broad and it has been applied to adopt a wide variety of legislative measures. Article 114 TFEU does, however, not provide for an unlimited competence for the EU to legislate (this would, for one, be contrary to the principle of conferred powers). In a ground-breaking decision, the *Tobacco Advertisement* case, the ECJ has indeed determined that this legal

---

3   And the ECJ sometimes relies on the preamble of legislative acts to decide on the legal basis. See P. Leino, 'The Institutional Politics of Objective Choice: Competence as a Framework for Argumentation', in S. Garben and I Govaere (eds), *The Division of Competences between the EU and the Member States. Reflections on the Past, the Present and the Future* (Portland: Hart Publishing, 2017).

4   Ibid.

basis may not serve as a general power to regulate the internal market. Rather, legislation based on this provision needs 'to actually contribute to eliminating obstacles to free movement and to removing distortions of competition'.[5]

The *Tobacco Advertisement* case concerned a classic conflict between Article 114 TFEU (EU competence) and national competences. It is precisely this type of competence conflict that we witness in the field of pensions, too. In this case, the directive at stake imposed a complete tobacco advertisement ban. As the EU treaties explicitly exclude public health from EU harmonization, the directive had been based on the internal market provision as the tobacco advertisement ban also related to the functioning of the internal market (e.g. the free movement of goods that contain tobacco advertisements). Nevertheless, the ECJ considered Article 114 TFEU to be incorrect and annulled the directive. The directive as a whole did not sufficiently improve the functioning of the internal market, according to the Court. The ECJ made, however, a specific distinction between elements that would be acceptable under Article 114 TFEU and other elements that would go beyond the scope thereof. One of the acceptable elements under Article 114 TFEU would be advertisements that are part of a more encompassing good or service. A ban on tobacco advertisements (in e.g. magazines) would foster the free movement of such magazines. The argument is that without such an EU-wide ban, magazines might be marketed in some Member States, whereas in others they might not be allowed on the market. The ECJ considered such aspects to be in line with Article 114 TFEU, as they would indeed contribute to the functioning of the internal market. Article 114 TFEU would only be inappropriate for those aspects of the directive for which no positive effects on the functioning of the internal market could be established. Following the ECJ's ruling, a new tobacco advertisement directive with a smaller scope was indeed adopted. Germany challenged this new directive as well, but this time the ECJ upheld it in line with the directions it had provided in the first decision.

The decision of the ECJ, focusing essentially on the effects of legislation, laid down a considerably different approach than the one it had previously applied. In older case law, the ECJ had formulated the so-called centre of gravity test to decide on competences issues. This test had been developed in the context of overlapping EU powers.[6] Notably, this case concerned a horizontal overlap of powers, i.e. both powers concerned EU competences

---

5   Case C-376/98, para. 95.
6   Case C-300/89.

but referred to different legislative procedures. The ECJ concluded that in such circumstances one legal basis should be the primary one and the 'centre of gravity' of the measure or its 'main purpose' should be the decisive factor in this regard. This involves a consideration of the concrete proposal and the available legal basis to assess what would be the best fit. It would have been a logical and consistent choice of the ECJ to apply the same test to vertical conflicts over competence. Indeed, this would have enhanced the constitutional nature of the EU as it would have entailed a balancing of constitutional interests (national and European ones). Such a centre of gravity test would also have reflected societal and political debates on the division of authority between the EU and the Member States better. The decision in the *Tobacco Advertisement* case, however, entails an outright rejection of the 'centre of gravity' test.[7]

This has important consequences. The EU legislature has no obligation to weigh national and EU competences to assess which competence would be most appropriate. Instead, it merely needs to assess whether the conditions for the application of the EU competence are fulfilled, without the need to consider whether perhaps a national competence is at issue and if so, how the internal market objectives relate to those national competences. The ECJ's approach entails, furthermore, a departure from the purpose of the measure as the key factor, to the foreseen effects thereof. Concretely, the main purpose of a measure based on Article 114 TFEU may be different from the promotion of internal market objectives, provided the proposed measure has positive effects on the functioning of the internal market.

Discussions among stakeholders and politicians on the role of the EU in regulating pensions have at times shown little understanding of the approach outlined above. At the time of the adoption of the first IORP Directive arguments were put forward such as that the Member States should retain 'full responsibility' for various aspects of pensions law.[8] Should the ECJ be requested to review the legality of EU pension legislation, such arguments would be treated as irrelevant. Indeed, as Davies argued, the division of competences in the EU is set up in such a way that the subject matter of legislation and the impact thereof on the Member States does not matter.[9]

---

7   D. Wyatt, 'Community Competence to Regulate the Internal Market', in M. Dougan and S. Currie (eds), *50 Years of European Treaties* (Portland: Hart Publishing, 2009).

8   See more elaborately: section 2.3.

9   G. Davies, 'Democracy and Legitimacy in the Shadow of Purposive Competence', *European Law Journal* 21.1 (2015).

Lenaerts, now president of the ECJ, observed in 1990 that 'no nucleus of sovereignty that the Member States can invoke, as such, [exists] against the Community'.[10] This is not a mere theoretical matter: as De Witte has demonstrated, a variety of EU legislative acts are in force which significantly impact areas which are in principle part of the national domain.[11]

Still, the application of Article 114 is not unlimited. The ECJ decided in the *Tobacco Advertisement* case that mere differences in national legislation, administrative practices etc. ('distortions' in the EU jargon) are insufficient to justify EU legislation. Such differences much indeed distort the functioning of the internal market. Article 114 TFEU requires that measures are adopted only to address distortions that are appreciable, whereas the proposed measures should make a positive contribution in overcoming these distortions and thereby contributing to a better functioning internal market. Article 114 TFEU may even be applied in case of future distortions, provided that it would be 'likely' that such distortions will indeed emerge.

It has been widely argued that the thresholds for applying Article 114 TFEU are indeed very low. Van Ooik already observed prior to the ECJ's ruling that it is hardly difficult to set up a reasoning in order to argue that differences in national legislation lead to inequalities in the market from which some may benefit and others suffer.[12] Weatherill concluded not only that the ECJ has never annulled EU legislation after the *Tobacco Advertisement* case for a wrongful legal basis, but also that the Court effectively provided the legislature with terminology and a vocabulary to be used to justify EU legislation.[13] If the EU legislature applies this vocabulary, the Court will not apply a stringent review of the legal basis.

It is no wonder that in this light Article 114 TFEU features prominently in debates on EU competence creep.[14] Admittedly, Article 352 TFEU is even broader in its scope. This provision creates a legal basis to adopt legislative

10   K. Lenaerts, 'Constitutionalism and the Many Faces of Federalism', *American Journal of Comparative Law* 38.2 (1990).

11   B. de Witte, 'Clarifying the Delimitation of Powers: A Proposal with Comments', in European Commission (ed.), *Europe 2004: Le Grand Débat: Setting the Agenda and Outlining the Options* (Brussels: European Commission, 2002).

12   R.H. van Ooik, *De keuze der rechtsgrondslag voor besluiten van de Europese Unie* (Deventer: Kluwer, 1999).

13   S. Weatherill, 'The Limits of Legislative Harmonisation Ten Years after Tobacco Advertising: How the Court's Case Law Has Become a "Drafting Guide"', *German Law Journal* 12.3 (2011).

14   S. Weatherill, 'Competence Creep and Competence Control', *Yearbook of European Law* 23.1 (2004).

measures to achieve 'objectives of the EU' if the treaties contain no more specific competences. Unanimity in the Council and other procedural guarantees, however, preclude it from being used too lightly. Indeed, legislative practice shows it is applied only rarely. This is different for Article 114 TFEU. Controversial applications of the provision include the setting up of financial agencies, such as EIOPA. In a case on EIOPA's sister agency ESMA (European Securities and Markets Authority), the UK argued that Article 114 TFEU had been breached as the legislative act at issue entrusted ESMA with single-case decision-making authority. The ECJ dismissed the argument and decided that the concept of harmonization encompasses not necessarily the adoption of generally applicable acts and need not necessarily pertain to national legislation.[15] The adoption of measures in the framework of the banking union (the single resolution mechanism) may be viewed as equally controversial as it applies to only a part of the EU (whereas the internal market encompasses the EU as a whole).

Although Article 114 TFEU may be the dominant legal basis for the regulation of pensions, some more provisions from the treaties should be considered here as well. Some of these legal bases exclude legislation and only allow for supporting measures. Such measures must then be restricted to soft law instruments and mechanisms such as the open method of coordination (OMC). Article 148 TFEU, on employment, gives the EU legislature (the Council, on a proposal from the Commission and after consulting the European Parliament) the competence to adopt guidelines which Member States are 'obliged to consider'. Articles 148(3) and (4) TFEU enable the Council to examine 'the implementation of the employment policies of the Member States in the light of the guidelines for employment' and to make recommendations to Member States. These provisions do not establish legal bases for the adoption of legislation *stricto sensu*, but may still have a significant impact on the Member States.[16]

More important, however, is the Economic and Monetary Union (EMU). Especially since the reforms of the EMU from 2011 onwards, the EMU has now a considerable potential to impact pension systems. The 'coordination of economic policies' concerns a competence that has been deliberately been kept outside of the so-called catalogue of competences which distinguishes

---

15   Case C-270/12.
16   Opinion on the legal basis of the proposal for a regulation of the European Parliament and of the Council on enforcement measures to correct excessive macroeconomic imbalances in the euro area, COM(2010) 525 – C7-0299/2010 – 2010/0279(COD), 12 April 2011.

between exclusive EU competences, shared competences and supportive/ coordination competences. This has in practice enabled a high level of flexibility.[17] Originally – and this is still how it emerges from the current Treaty of Lisbon – broad economic policy guidelines (BEPGs) should be the main instrument to coordinate economic policies. These BEPGs are essentially well-argued recommendations. However, since 2011 a new system of economic policy coordination has been established under the umbrella of the 'European Semester'. This system is based on a set of legislative measures and an intergovernmental treaty: the Treaty on Stability, Coordination and Governance.[18] This is not the place for an in-depth analysis of the complex institutional set-up of the European Semester.[19] For the purposes of this contribution it suffices to mention that it consists of a structured policy dialogue between EU and national actors. National governments adopt budgetary and economic plans and the EU responds by issuing country-specific recommendations (CSRs) to the Member States. Ultimately, ignoring these recommendations may result in the imposition of financial sanctions. Thus, for the Member States the European Semester is a more binding system than terms such as 'policy dialogue' and 'recommendations' suggest. The European Semester covers budgetary and fiscal policies, but also economic performance policies.

National pension systems may be affected by both policies of the European Semester. The former policy is at stake in as far as pension systems have consequences for national public finances. More importantly, however, economic performance policies cover all policies of the Member States that impact the functioning of the national economy. Thereby, pension systems may be addressed in the framework of the European Semester if the functioning of these systems affect economic objectives underlying EU economic performance policies. The current policy practice demonstrates that this may include a myriad of economic objectives, such as economic growth and economic stability, competitiveness, convergence (of economies

---

17   T. van den Brink, 'Op zoek naar soevereiniteit in de EMU: EU economisch beleid en de verhoudingen tussen de EU en de lidstaten', in S. Hardt, A.W. Heringa, A. Waltermann (eds), *Bevrijdende en begrenzende soevereiniteit* (Maastricht: Boom, 2018).

18   K. Armstrong, 'The New Governance of EU Fiscal Discipline', *European Law Review* 38.5 (2013) ; F. Amtenbrink, 'Legal Developments', *Journal of Common Market Studies* 50 (2012). On the Stability, Coordination and Governance Treaty, see P.P. Craig, 'The Stability, Coordination and Governance Treaty: Principle, Politics and Pragmatism', *European Law Review* 37.3 (2012).

19   For a more detailed elaboration, see T. van den Brink, 'National Parliaments and EU Economic Performance Policies: Impact Defines Involvement?', *Journal of European Integration* 40.3 (2018).

in Europe), preventing and addressing so-called 'macroeconomic imbalances' and even social objectives.[20]

A concrete and striking example concerns the recommendations on the pension system that have been addressed to the Netherlands. The Dutch pension system is generally seen as unique in the EU and hailed for its benefits. Yet, this has not prevented EU institutions to point out several weaknesses of the system and calling upon the Dutch government to address these.[21] Especially the need to make the pension system fairer in terms of a better inter- and intra-generational distribution of costs and benefits has been voiced recurrently.[22] In 2015, the CSRs included a specific recommendation to reduce the level of contributions to the second pillar of the pension system for those in the early years of their working life. In 2018, the Dutch pension system was still high on the Commission's agenda.[23] Apart from the need to make the system fairer, the Commission considered that the pension system should be made more transparent and more resilient to shocks. On the latter point, the Commission added the ageing of the population should be better taken into account.

The EMU presents the EU institutions with a new, and potentially more direct, way to impact the design and functioning of national pension systems. The justification for EU action is derived from the impact of pension systems on the performance of national economies. The form of action is different from legislation, but the country-specific approach allows for tailor-made – and thereby potentially also more intrusive – EU policies. Together with the internal market competences the EU institutions are thus equipped with ample competences to adopt measures that affect national pension systems. Whether the EU institutions indeed use these competences is obviously a different issue and depends greatly on political will. However, the exercise of EU competences depends not only on political will but is also subject to the principles of subsidiarity and proportionality.

20 Van den Brink 2018, fn 56.

21 For more detail on the CSRs for 2014-2015, see Van den Brink, 2018, fn 58, section 3.2.

22 In 2018 this recommendation was included in the CSR for the Netherlands: European Commission, 'Recommendation for a Council Recommendation on the 2018 National Reform Programme of the Netherlands and Delivering a Council Opinion on the 2018 Stability Programme of the Netherlands', COM(2018) 418 final, 23 March 2018, https://ec.europa.eu/info/sites/info/files/file_import/2018-european-semester-country-specific-recommendation-commission-recommendation-netherlands-en.pdf.

23 Ibid.

2.3   The exercise of EU competences: The principles of subsidiarity and proportionality

2.3.1   Subsidiarity

The principle of subsidiarity demands that EU policy objectives should be achieved at the lowest level of governance. If national or even sub-national action would be effective to achieve EU policy objectives, the EU itself should refrain from adopting legislation or other measures. Article 5(3) TEU reads as follows:

> [T]he Union shall act only if and in so far as the objectives of the proposed action cannot be sufficiently achieved by the Member States, either at central level or at regional and local level, but can rather, by reason of the scale or effects of the proposed action, be better achieved at Union level.

Thus, the subsidiarity principle requires what has been labelled a 'national insufficiency test' and a 'comparative efficiency test'.[24] Especially in areas – such as that of pensions law – which are considered to fall between EU objectives and national interests, the subsidiarity principle plays an important role. In protecting the Member States against over-intrusive EU action, the subsidiarity principle is often viewed as a manifestation of national sovereignty. This view, however, risks overburdening subsidiarity with expectations that go well beyond the limits of its capacity. Indeed, Article 5 TEU entails that the subsidiarity principle comes into play when the existence of an EU policy objective and a corresponding competence has already been established. Thus, the subsidiarity principle serves as a principle to decide which level is of government is the best to achieve EU objectives, rather than as a principle to balance national and EU interests or as a weapon to successfully challenge EU competences. It is exactly for this reason that Davies criticized subsidiarity and considered it an inappropriate tool to protect the Member States.[25] Still, the introduction of subsidiarity (the principle achieved treaty status with the Maastricht Treaty) was seen by various scholars and others as a threat to the EU. Toth described it as a

---

24 K. Lenaerts, 'Subsidiarity and Community Competence in the Field of Education', *Columbia Journal of European Law* 1.1 (1994).
25 G. Davies, Subsidiarity: The Wrong Idea, in the Wrong Place, at the Wrong Time', *Common Market Law Review* 43.1 (2006).

'retrograde step' and predicted it would 'weaken the Community and slow down the integration process'.[26]

Nevertheless, the Treaty of Lisbon[27] reinforced subsidiarity in the following ways:[28]

–   By making the legally binding nature of the principle for all EU institutions and for all of their acts explicit (Article 1 of the protocol)
–   The system of monitoring the application of subsidiarity by national parliaments (Articles 4-7 of the protocol) known as the Early Warning Mechanism
–   The review by the ECJ of legislative acts' compliance with the principle of subsidiarity (Article 8 of the protocol)

The first and third aspect were in fact not new, but the explicit inclusion in the text of the protocol is not merely symbolic. As will be demonstrated later, the ECJ takes a more substantive interpretation of the principle, which may well be attributed to the treaty amendment. What is new about the ECJ's review of subsidiarity is that Member States' parliaments have been granted the right to challenge legislation on the basis of subsidiarity before the Court. The second aspect, the involvement of national parliaments in scrutinizing subsidiarity, entailed an institutional innovation, as it formally introduced national parliaments in the EU legislative process. Their role is, however, not fully legislative, as they lack the competence to block or amend legislative proposals of the Commission. However, when a sufficient number of national parliaments object by sending the Commission a reasoned opinion, the Commission will be obliged to reconsider its proposal. Moreover, the Commission engages with (individual) national parliaments in the framework of the so-called political dialogue.

The recast of the IORP Directive has led to action by national parliaments based on the post-Lisbon institutional position of national parliaments.[29] In a reasoned opinion, the Dutch House of Representatives argued that

26   A.G. Toth, 'The Principle of Subsidiarity in the Maastricht Treaty', *Common Market Law Review* 29.6 (1992).
27   The relevant provisions are to be found in the Subsidiarity and Proportionality Protocol.
28   For more information, see Ton van den Brink, 'Towards an Ever Clearer Division of Authority between the European Union and the Member States?', in T. van den Brink, M, Luchtman, M, Scholten (eds), *Sovereignty in the Shared Legal Order of the EU: Core Values of Regulation and Enforcement* (Antwerpen: Intersentia, 2015).
29   The Dutch parliament sent a reasoned opinion and a political dialogue took place with the Italian, Portuguese and Romanian parliaments.

the Commission's proposal violated subsidiarity.[30] It argued that pension systems concern national 'responsibilities and competences' and that the Commission had insufficiently substantiated what the added value of the proposal would be. This approach to subsidiarity reflected the way in which the principle had already featured in the decision-making process on the first IORP Directive. This resulted in the inclusion of the following text (Recital 9) in the IORP I Directive:

> In accordance with the principle of subsidiarity, Member States should retain full responsibility for the organisation of their pension systems as well as for the decision on the role of each of the three 'pillars' of the second pillar, they should also retain full responsibility for the role and functions of the various institutions providing occupational retirement benefits, such as industry-wide pension funds, company pension funds and life-assurance companies. This Directive is not intended to call this prerogative into question.

In the IORP II Directive, this wording has remained largely unchanged (now Recital 19). By using the subsidiarity principle to argue that these aspects of pension regulation need to remain at the national level, the EU legislature (and the Dutch parliament as well) demonstrates a misinterpretation of the principle. This is not in line with the treaty definition as elaborated above and would not hold before the ECJ. Indeed, the argumentation fits better in the context of the principle of conferral as it considers that two aspects should a priori be excluded from EU competence, i.e. the organization of pension system and the balancing of the three pension pillars.[31] The problem with such a reasoning is obviously that the notion that national areas can be ring-fenced in order to remain immune to EU interference simply has not been acknowledged in the EU system of division of competences.

The Commission's reply to the Dutch parliament's reasoned opinion reflected an understanding of subsidiarity which is more in line with the treaty interpretation.[32] Admittedly, the Commission referred to the consideration (included in the above-quoted recital) that several aspects of pension regulation should remain national, such as the organization of pension systems and in particular

---

30 Letter of 15 May 2014, available (in Dutch) at http://www.ipex.eu/IPEXL-WEB/scrutiny/COD20140091/nltwe.do.

31 Scrutiny of legislative proposals in light of the conferral principle is a common element of national parliaments' reasoned opinions: K. Granat, *The Principle of Subsidiarity and Its Enforcement in the EU Legal Order: The Role of National Parliaments in the Early Warning System* (London: Bloomsbury, 2018), ch. 3.

32 European Commission, letter of 25 July 2014, C(2014) 5427.

the decision on the role which occupational pensions play in that system and about the social and labour law provisions applicable to occupational pensions. The Commission subsequently put forward some typical subsidiarity arguments, however. It referred to the internal market objective underlying the directive and stated that the directive entails no full harmonization of IORPs but remains limited to provisions that seek to remove obstacles to cross-border activities of IORPs. Cross-border IORP activities may lead to efficiency gains and may thereby contribute to further develop occupational pensions within the EU, which would be impossible for the Member States to achieve individually. Furthermore, the directive would, according to the Commission, ensure a level playing field between IORP providers from different Member States and will therefore avoid the situation in which IORPs engage in regulatory arbitrage and dislocate to Member States that have not introduced high standards.

Apart from efficiency gains and the creation of a level playing field the Commission argued that the proposal would respect national diversity. By regulating only specific elements of pension provision – elements where 'the EU could add the most value and reinforce the policy actions by individual Member States' – the proposal would remain far from full harmonization and would respect the specific nature and the importance of occupational retirement provision within the Dutch and other pension systems.

Whereas the Commission thus reflected a better understanding of subsidiarity, the treaties give little guidance on which substantive criteria should be applied. The new protocol is silent on this issue, which is remarkable in light of the increased significance of the principle. Moreover, the old protocol did contain substantive elements. It included the following criteria:[33]

- The existence of transnational aspects
- Abstaining from Community measures would conflict with the requirements of the treaty or would otherwise significantly damage Member States' interests
- Community measures would produce clear benefits by reason of its scale or effects

These criteria are essentially still the only criteria that can be derived from the EU's constitutional system.[34] The Interinstitutional Agreement between the European Parliament, the Council of the European Union

33   These indicators were derived from the conclusions of the European Council of Edinburgh of 11-12 December 1992.
34   Granat, *The Principle of Subsidiarity*, ch. 3.

and the European Commission on Better Law-Making (IIA) contains no additional or more refined criteria, but only underscores the importance of the principle in general terms.[35] A more recent report, commissioned by Commission Vice-President Timmermans and drafted by the Task Force on Subsidiarity, Proportionality and 'Doing Less More Efficiently', also did not add much.[36] Even though one of the objectives of the task force was to come to 'a better understanding' of the principle. The Task force did propose to adopt a 'subsidiarity assessment grid', but considered that a more elaborate assessment grid could be incorporated in a future revision of the IIA.[37] The elements of the grid proposed by the task force included some questions to further flesh out the following elements of the tests:

- The scale of the issue (most notably degree in which transnational/ cross-border aspects are at stake);
- Diversity (in the way in which the issue plays out in the Member States, in views of how the issue should be tackled);
- Added value of EU action (benefits of EU action, e.g. by efficiency gains and legal clarity, but also – interestingly – by weighing the benefits of EU action against the loss of national autonomy).

The foreseen course of action for the Task force would be a further refinement of these elements and particularly a more consistent and rigorous application thereof, including in the context of reviewing of existing legislation.

Meanwhile, the role of the ECJ has remained extremely limited, despite subsidiarity being a legally binding principle of EU law. As Granat explained, the Court has adopted essentially two main approaches.[38] The first is a procedural one and essentially requires that subsidiarity must have been considered by the legislature. This test has existed for a longer time, but has been intensified in the post-Lisbon period. The ECJ now requires the EU legislature to produce sufficient subsidiarity justification through evidence and impact assessments. The second test is a substantive one and looks at the cross-border nature of the issue that the legislative act seeks to address. This test is of a younger date and has been developed through the *Vodafone* case. In this case the ECJ examined the legality of the Roaming Regulation, in particular the provisions on retail

35   Interinstitutional Agreement between the European Parliament, the Council of the European Union and the European Commission on Better Law-Making of 12 May 2016, OJ L 123.
36   Report available from https://ec.europa.eu/commission/priorities/democratic-change/ better-regulation/task-force-subsidiarity-proportionality-and-doing-less-more-efficiently_nl.
37   At. p. 12.
38   Granat, *The Principle of Subsidiarity*, ch. 3.

prices for mobile telephone services.[39] The ECJ concluded that perhaps retail prices in itself would have little cross-border significance, but argued that retail and wholesale charges were highly interdependent (for the latter, the cross-border aspect was much stronger). Furthermore, regulation of both aspects at the EU level would imply that operators would be allowed to act within a single coherent regulatory framework. Thus, the regulation complied with subsidiarity, but it was for the first time the ECJ came to such a conclusion based on an independent substantive reasoning. The cross-border nature of the issue has since become the key substantive criterion for the Court.

What are the consequences of all this for the possible development of EU pension legislation? Subsidiarity concerns from Member States' parliaments will have the greatest impact when such concerns are shared by a sufficient number of parliaments to trigger a yellow card. The isolated position of the Dutch parliament in case of the IORP revision resulted in a total lack of impact on the final outcome. In such circumstances, the option to challenge the legislative act before the ECJ is available. Given the limited substantive review, such a claim will, however, not easily be accepted by the Court. A lack of substantial evidence to justify compliance with the principle will provide better chances of success.

2.3.2 Proportionality

The principles of subsidiarity and proportionality are related in that they both concern the exercise of EU powers. They are, however, distinct. Proportionality regards the question how an issue should be regulated rather than the question at which level.[40] Article 5(4) TEU reads: 'Under the principle of proportionality, the *content* and *form* of Union action shall not exceed what is necessary to achieve the objectives of the Treaties' (emphasis added).

The principle offers a broad scope of protection. As a general principle of EU law, it applies to all EU actions. Equally broad are the interests which the principle seeks to protect. First, as in other legal systems, proportionality protects individuals against over-intrusive actions of public authority (e.g. abuse of discretion).[41] The EU proportionality principle has a broader scope, however. It not only regulates the relation between the private and the public, but includes protection of Member States' sovereignty as well. As the principle of subsidiarity offers Member States only protection regarding the

---

39 Case C-58/08.
40 See Granat, *The Principle of Subsidiarity*, ch. 3.
41 P.P. Craig, *Administrative Law*, 5th ed. (London: Sweet & Maxwell, 2003).

most suitable level of regulation, other aspects – such as the intensity of EU regulation and the degree of national discretion – may only be protected under the proportionality principle.

A commonly accepted definition of proportionality distinguishes three elements:[42]

- The measure must be suitable to attain a legitimate aim
- The measure must be necessary (which involves a verification whether there were no equally efficient but less onerous means available)
- Proportionality is interpreted in the narrow sense: whether the measure entails no disproportionate interference of other interests, e.g. the rights and freedoms of individuals

Some important observations must be drawn from this definition. First, proportionality requires a strong connection between the objective of a measure and the measure itself. All aspects of the latter must be viewed in light of the objective(s) of the measure. This creates restraints, but it also focuses the legislature. Second, the last element of the definition requires a balancing of interests and policy objectives in the light of the concrete content of the measure. This requires the legislature to identify which other policy objectives and individual rights and interests are affected by the measure.

Otherwise, the scholarly attention for this definition has focused mainly on the intensity of judicial review. Especially the third element is problematic in this regard, as it is the least objective of the three and it risks the Court putting itself in the legislature's place. Nevertheless, the relevance of proportionality stretches well beyond the issue of judicial review. There are more concrete elements for the EU legislature to consider in the application of subsidiarity. The current (aforementioned) Subsidiarity and Proportionality Protocol requires the legislature to minimize and commensurate financial and administrative burdens on the EU, national governments, regional or local authorities, economic operators and citizens.[43] The old Subsidiarity and Proportionality Protocol contained more substantive guidance for the legislature. It included the following concrete elements:

- Directives should be preferred over regulations
- Framework directives should be preferred over detailed measures

---

42   This definition is founded on the decision of the CJEU in the *Fedesa* case, in which it distinguished these three elements explicitly: Case C-331/88.
43   Article 5 of the protocol.

- The EU legislature should leave as much scope for national decision as possible;
- Care should be taken to respect well-established national arrangements and the organization and working of Member States' legal systems;
- If possible, EU measures should provide Member States with alternative ways to achieve the objectives of the measures.

The old protocol thereby strongly underscored the substantive aspects of proportionality. A more procedural side of proportionality is the central point of the Interinstitutional Agreement between the European Parliament, the Council of the European Union and the European Commission on Better Law-Making. Key element thereof is the obligation to carry out impact assessments (IAs). IAs should include detailed information on the 'existence, scope and consequences' of the problem that the proposed legislation seeks to address and map out the effects of the proposed measure as well as alternatives thereto. When assessing these effects, in particular the impact on competitiveness and administrative burdens (thereby reflecting the current treaty protocol), digital aspects and territorial impact.[44]

IAs thus contribute to informed, and thereby rationalized, decision-making. As such, they are functional to – and indeed indispensable for – a better quality of proportionality assessments. The revision of the IORP Directive has been preceded by an IA that highlights several proportionality elements.[45] First, it includes four specific problems for which the revision is necessary:

- Cross-border activity is still expensive and complex for employers, which prevents IORPs from benefiting from the internal market;
- Insufficient guarantees that those who effectively manage IORPs act in the best interest of the scheme members or beneficiaries;
- Information inefficiencies arising from a lack of clear and effective communication
- Supervisory powers are insufficient to effectively ensure that IORPs comply with the prudential standards and information disclosures.

---

44   No. 12 of the IIA.

45   European Commission, Impact Assessment Accompanying the Document Proposal for a Directive of the European Parliament and of the Council on the Activities and Supervision of Institutions for Occupational Retirement Provision, SWD(2014) 103 final, 27 March 2014, https:// eur-lex.europa.eu/resource.html?uri=cellar:d2808315-b690-11e3-86f9-01aa75ed71a1.0001.01/ DOC_1&format=PDF.

Further on, the Commission focuses on the third element of the proportionality assessment as elaborated by the ECJ where it identifies the other interests at stake: apart from the public interest, the protection of IORP members and beneficiaries, as well as the costs for IORPs, sponsoring employers and supervisors. The Commission then points at how the proposal takes a limited approach for concrete elements such as regarding new supervisory powers.[46] The quality of this IA has been criticized, however, by the Commission's own Impact Assessment Board, which oversees the quality of the IAs carried out. Also the UK House of Commons has been critical on the proposal, especially on proportionality grounds.[47] It pointed at the limited cross-border aspect of IORPs (and the limited potential that the cross-border activities of IORPs would increase), the administrative burdens involved and the diverse role that occupational pensions play in overall pension provision. The Council and the European Parliament (EP) were less critical and eventually agreed on a compromise text, but they have, nevertheless, wanted to introduce less intrusive and less far-reaching provisions on various points.[48] This may be viewed as proportionality adaptations to the Commission's proposal. Thus, the revision of the IORP Directive demonstrates the substantial role of the proportionality principle in legislative procedures; first and foremost in substantive terms (impacting the content of legislation) but this is strongly stimulated by the IA requirement as well (which may be seen as a manifestation of procedural proportionality).

2.4   Legislation and administrative rule-making

2.4.1   Introduction

A fierce dispute in EU pensions law regards the issue which aspects – if any – may be left to the Commission to regulate. Essentially, this entails the question how EU legislation should be delineated from administrative rule-making which is a common issue in most legal systems. Less controversial, more technical rules are usually left to institutions of the executive branch,

46   Ibid.

47   European Scrutiny Committee, report, 4 June 2014, https://www.parliament.uk/documents/commons-committees/european-scrutiny/Sefcovic-35944-1.pdf.

48   A insightful overview thereof is provided by a European Parliament briefing of January 2017: 'Occupational Pensions: Revision of the Institutions for Occupational Retirement Provision Directive (IORP II)', http://www.europarl.europa.eu/RegData/etudes/BRIE/2017/595899/EPRS_BRI(2017)595899_EN.pdf.

in order for parliamentary institutions to be able to focus on (and reserve their scarce resources to) matters of the highest political importance. This applies to the European Union as well. The volume of executive rule-making also in the EU far exceeds that of legislation in a true sense.

The first observation that should be made here is of a terminological nature. The use of the term 'legislation' is often cause of confusion. It is regularly used as an umbrella term for all legal acts which include generally applicable legal norms. This broad definition is similar to the popular use of the term, in which e.g. EU pensions legislation denotes all generally applicable norms in the field, regardless of their origin. In the EU, however, a procedural notion of legislation prevails. This denotes a more limited notion of legislation, i.e. parliamentary legislation, thereby excluding all forms of executive rule-making. Unfortunately, the EU's typology for the latter is 'non-legislative acts', although these acts may indeed concern legislation in the substantive sense.

The EU legislative system includes further peculiarities, such as the subdivision of non-legislative acts into delegated and implementing acts and comitology. These and other characteristics are key for how pensions may be – and effectively are – regulated at the EU level and for understanding how EU pensions legislation may impact the Member States.

In this section, we will elaborate the main characteristics of the EU's legislative system and assess the implications thereof on EU pensions law.

2.4.2   Distinguishing legislative and non-legislative acts

The prime responsibility for adopting generally binding rules lies with the legislature. This principle, a common feature of legal systems based on the *trias politica* and the rule of law, applies to the EU legislature as well. The strong legitimacy basis of the EU legislature – consisting of the European Commission, the Council of Ministers and the European Parliament – ensures democratic, Member States' and European interests to be represented in decision-making procedures. Thus, legislation is hierarchically superior to administrative rule-making and the latter needs to be based on a specific enabling clause from an EU legislative act.

Articles 288-292 TFEU provide the general framework for legislative acts and administrative rule-making. The central feature is the distinction between 'legislative' or 'non-legislative' acts.[49] Article 289 TFEU is the govern-

---

49   C.F. Bergström, D. Ritleng, 'Introduction', in C.F. Bergström, D. Ritleng (eds), *Rulemaking by the EU Commission: The New System of Delegation of Powers* (Oxford: Oxford Scholarship Online, 2016).

ing provision on legislative acts. According to this provision, legislative acts are legal acts that are adopted by a legislative procedure. The content and form of the act (these may be regulations, directives, or decisions) is not relevant – when an act is adopted by the legislative procedure it constitutes a legislative act.[50] Non-legislative acts may be acts of single case decision-making acts or, for the purposes of this contribution more relevant, acts of administrative rule-making. Non-legislative acts find their legal basis, as said, in a legislative act. The EU legislator thus defines the scope of administrative rule-making. Nonetheless, the freedom of the EU legislature to delegate rule-making authority has limits. Article 290 TFEU provides that the EU legislature may only delegate the adoption of 'non-essential elements' to the Commission. This limitation also applies to the adoption of implementing acts (Article 291 TFEU).[51] Thus, 'essential elements' – which must be the responsibility of the EU legislature itself – and 'non-essential elements' – which may be left to executive institutions – should be sharply distinguished.

Especially in the adoption of the IORP Directive (and in its revision) the issue of the scope of executive rule-making featured prominently. It is important to understand, however, that the decision which elements are essential is not entirely in the hands of the EU's legislative institutions. The ECJ effectively scrutinizes legislative acts and may assess whether essential elements have erroneously been delegated to the Commission or the Council. In a decision on the Schengen Borders Code the ECJ made clear that the findings as to which elements are essential are to be 'based on objective factors amenable to judicial review' (para. 67).[52] According to the ECJ, the decision of the Council supplementing the Schengen Borders Code (in the form of what we would now refer to as an implementing act) did indeed involve essential elements. Said elements should have been laid down in the basic act and the decision of the Council therefore had to be annulled. The essential elements that should have been regulated at the legislative level included notably the enforcement powers granted to border guards to take coercive measures.

The ECJ argued that these elements were to be considered 'essential' for two main reasons. They affected – and limited – the protection of

<hr>

50 P. Craig, G. de Búrca, *EU Law: Text, Cases, and Materials*, 6th ed. (Oxford: Oxford University Press, 2016).

51 The rule that secondary normative measures in general may only concern non-essential elements was originally formulated in the *Köster* case, Case C-25/70.

52 Case C-355/10, para. 76.

fundamental rights and they entailed 'political choices'. This latter point meant that the norms adopted had been the outcome of a balance between conflicting interests, *in casu* the protection of the migrant versus effective policing of the EU's external borders. It is difficult even in the case of highly technical executive rules to fully exclude the possibility that such norms are to some extent a compromise between conflicting interests. The ECJ, indeed, applies this criterion not very strictly,[53] but it is important for EU legislative institutions to still consider this as an outer limit to the delegation of rule-making authority to the executive.[54] This is particularly so in the case of outright conflicts between political or legal interests.

Nevertheless, the decision of the ECJ sheds little light on what 'essential elements' exactly are.[55] It has been argued that the ECJ missed an opportunity to clarify the dividing line between essential and non-essential elements.[56] Moreover, the ECJ is inconsistent in its approach: in some cases it scrutinizes delegated or implementing acts on whether they contain essential elements, in other cases the Court examines the legislative act itself.[57] It has thus also been argued to come to a more structured approach, which would entail an assessment of both acts and their interrelation.[58]

The power of the ECJ to delineate legislative acts from non-legislative acts also impacts the relations between institutions. A good example is the ECJ's ruling on a decision of the Commission to withdraw a proposal for a regulation on macro-financial assistance to third countries.[59] The EU legislative procedure is based upon a particular understanding of the institutional balance between the three legislative institutions. The European Commission has the exclusive right of legislative initiative, but is not

53   M. Chamon, 'Limits to Delegation under Article 290 TFEU: The Specificity and Essentiality Requirements Put to the Test', *Maastricht Journal of European and Comparative Law* 25.2 (2018).

54   Den Heyer and Tauschinsky, in particular, highlighted fundamental rights issues as a limit to delegation: M. den Heijer, E. Tauschinsky, 'Where Human Rights Meet Administrative Law: Essential Elements and Limits to Delegation: European Court of Justice, Grand Chamber C-355/10: *European Parliament v Council of the European Union*', *European Constitutional Law Review* 9.3 (2013).

55   K. Bradley, 'Delegation of Powers in the European Union', in C.F. Bergström and D. Ritleng (eds), *Rulemaking by the EU Commission: the New System of Delegation of Powers* (Oxford: Oxford Scholarship Online, 2016).

56   M. Chamon, 'How the Concept of Essential Elements of a Legislative Act Continues to Elude the Court', *Common Market Law Review* 50.3 (2013).

57   The decision of the Tribunal in Case T-630/13, *DK Recycling und Roheisen*, ECLI:EU:C:2014:833 is an example of the latter.

58   Chamon, 'Limits to Delegation under Article 290 TFEU'.

59   Case C-409/13.

involved (at least not formally) in the adoption of legislation. By contrast, the EP and the Council formally adopt legislation but are dependent on the Commission to issue proposals. In this case the Commission disapproved of how the EP and the Council had amended the proposal. In particular, it disagreed with the removal of an implementing power which would grant the Commission the power to decide on the actual conferral of assistance. It decided to withdraw the proposal, thereby making it impossible for the other institutions to adopt the legislative act. In the procedure before the ECJ these institutions argued that decisions on granting assistance involved essential elements and should thus be adopted by the legislature. The ECJ disagreed with that view. It considered that one of the main objectives of the proposal was to accelerate the decision-making on providing assistance. In light thereof, the implementing power was to be considered an essential element of the proposal.[60]

The division of labour between the EU legislature and the Commission has been a key issue in the revision process of the IORP Directive (2014-2016) as well. The initial proposal contained various provisions to delegate rule-making authority to the Commission.[61] Examples were Article 24 (on remuneration policy), Article 30 on risk assessment and evaluation and Article 54 (on the pension benefit statement). Following criticism from both academics[62] and stakeholders,[63] these provisions were deleted from the final text of the directive. Such criticism included arguments that the delegation provisions at issue were drafted with an insufficient degree of specificity and left 'too many issues that are of vital importance to the architecture of the regulation outside the ordinary legislative process'. Essentially, such criticism questioned whether these delegation provisions respected the constitutional limits on delegation and implementation. These limits will be further examined in the next sub-section. Meanwhile, the discussion on delegating rule-making authority to the Commission has not ended. In Spring 2018, the Commission has adopted a series of legislative proposals on sustainable finance, including on improving disclosure requirements on how institutional investors integrate environmental, social and governance (ESG) factors in their risk processes. One of the proposals entails an amendment of the IORP Directive to grant the European Commission delegating authority

---

60   Para. 91 of the decision.
61   Proposal for a Directive on the activities and supervision of institutions for occupational retirement provision (recast), COM/2014/0167 final.
62   N. Moloney, *EU Securities and Financial Markets Regulation* (Oxford: Oxford EU Law Library, 2014).
63   Opinion of the Economic and Social Committee, 2012/C 191/15.

to adopt delegated acts that ensure that IORPs actually include ESG factors and risks in investment decisions and risk-management processes as a way to implement the 'prudent person' rule.[64]

2.4.3 Delegation and implementation

Already before the Treaty of Lisbon, it had proved to be difficult to make a clear distinction between legislative and non-legislative acts. The European Convention, which paved the way for the eventual Treaty of Lisbon, included a working group dealing specifically with the issue. It proposed a typology consisting of three types of legal acts.[65] This proposal has been incorporated in the Treaty of Lisbon in the sense that apart from legislative acts two other categories of legal acts are now to be distinguished: delegated and implementing acts. Delegated acts, although formally non-legislative in nature, must be viewed as a category between the pure technical category of implementing acts on the one hand and legislative acts on the other.[66]

According to Article 290 TFEU, delegated acts are acts of general application to supplement or amend certain non-essential elements of the parent legislative act. The legislative act must define – in the delegating provision – the objectives, content, scope, and duration of the delegation of power. Contrary to many national legal systems, the EU legislature is thus subject to constitutional requirements and limits. The definitions of 'amending' and 'supplementing' are crucial: to 'amend' is defined as making formal changes to the parent legislative act (deleting, replacing or adding non-essential elements), whereas to 'supplement' concerns the addition of new non-essential rules or norms to the regulatory framework. By contrast, the 'implementation' of legislative acts, the subject matter of Article 291 TFEU, is meant to give effect to rules that have been laid down in the basic legislative act and consequently does not entail the establishment of new rules or norms are established.[67]

---

64 Proposal for a Regulation on Disclosures Relating to Sustainable Investments and Sustainability Risks and Amending Directive (EU) 2016/2341, COM(2018) 354 final. The proposed regulation would amend Article 19 of the directive to this end.

65 Final Report of Working Group IX on Simplification of 29 November 2002, CONV 424/02, http://europeanconvention.europa.eu; Bergström and Ritleng, 'Introduction'.

66 Craig and De Búrca, *EU Law*.

67 EU Commission, Implementing of the Treaty of Lisbon. Delegated Acts. Guidelines for the Services of the Commission (Brussels, 2011); T. Christiansen and M. Dobbels, 'Non-Legislative Rule Making after the Lisbon Treaty: Implementing the New System of Comitology and Delegated Acts', *European Law Journal* 19.1 (2013).

This brings us to the definition of implementing acts. According to Article 291 TFEU, implementing acts are acts that ensure that legally binding European Union acts are implemented subject to uniform conditions.[68] Strikingly, the definitions of delegated acts and implementing acts are thus unrelated.[69] Whereas delegated acts are defined on the basis of their scope of application (supplementing or amending non-essential elements of legislative acts), the definition of implementing acts is based on their function and rationale (implementing acts allow legislative acts to be applied according to uniform conditions).[70] Thus, delegated and implementing acts are not mutually exclusive.[71] The key difference with delegated acts is that implementing acts execute the parent act without amendment or supplementation.[72] However, there is a problem with the Commission's approach outlined above that implementing acts do not entail the establishment of new norms. The creation of uniform conditions for the execution of legislative acts will to some degree always involve 'adding something' to the parent act. Still, fleshing out the provisions of legislative acts in greater detail may be seen as the core of implementing acts whereas if supplementation or even amending the parent act is required, recourse should be had to Article 290 TFEU.[73]

More explicit are the differences in institutional and procedural terms. The Council and the European Parliament have strong powers to control the adoption of delegated acts. These so-called call-back rights allow these institutions to object to a specific delegated act[74] or even to revoke the delegation provision itself (thus taking away the Commission's power to adopt delegated acts altogether).[75] By contrast, implementing acts are subject

---

68   By exception, and unlike delegated acts, also the Council may be entrusted with implementing powers.

69   Christiansen and Dobbels, 'Non-Legislative Rule Making'.

70   European Commission, Commission Communication: Implementing Article 290 of the Treaty on the European Union, COM(2009) 673 final.

71   J. Bast, 'Is There a Hierarchy of Legislative, Delegated, and Implementing Acts?', in C.F. Bergström and D. Ritleng (eds), *Rulemaking by the EU Commission: The New System of Delegation of Powers* (Oxford: Oxford Scholarship Online, 2016).

72   Craig and De Búrca, *EU Law*.

73   Ibid.

74   A couple of examples: the Council has raised an objection against a delegated act of the Commission of 12 August 2014 regarding the format for submitting data on expenses for research and developments as referred to in Regulation (EU) 549/2013 on the European system of national and regional accounts in the European Union. In 2014, the European Parliament objected to a delegated regulation of the Commission regarding the definition of 'technically manufactured nanomaterials' that was based on Regulation (EU) 1169/2011 on the provision of food information to consumers.

75   Article 290(2) TFEU.

to the system of 'committee procedures' or 'comitology'.[76] This entails the *ex ante* involvement of national experts with varying degrees of power. Delegated acts therefore carry more weight as they are subject to stronger supervision by the other institutions.[77] Yet, the treaties have not established a formal hierarchy between delegated and implementing acts.[78] The differences between the two seem more gradual than fundamental. Indeed, the argument by Schütze, to put delegation in the realm of the legislature and implementation within the scope of the executive, is unconvincing.[79] His argument is based on the applicable control mechanisms: delegation relies on democratic guarantees and implementation – by contrast – on control by the Member States. Such a fundamental difference between delegation and implementation is hardly reflected in the EU's legislative practice. In terms of content, delegated and implementing acts often hardly differ.[80] Moreover, whereas implementation is supposed to only give effect to existing provisions of primary legislation (and, thus, to refrain from adding new elements thereto), the reality is that it inevitably often involves value judgements and political choices.[81]

The ECJ has shed light on the distinction between delegation and implementation, but only some.[82] It has primarily stressed the political discretion of the legislative institutions and limited itself to noting that 'the purpose of delegating a legislative power is to achieve the adoption of rules coming from the regulatory framework as defined by the basic legislative act' whereas,

'when the EU legislature confers an implementing power on the Commission on the basis of Article 291(2) TFEU, the Commission is called on to provide further detail in relation to the content of a legislative act, in order to ensure that it is implemented under uniform conditions in all Member States'.[83]

---

76   Article 291(3) TFEU.

77   An additional argument can be found in the fact that the concept of the delegated act had to replace the most far-reaching type of committee procedure, i.e. the regulatory procedure with scrutiny (known under its French acronym PRAC).

78   J. Bast, 'New Categories of Acts after the Lisbon Reform: Dynamics of Parliamentarization in EU Law', *Common Market Law Review* 49.3 (2012).

79   R. Schütze, '"Delegated" Legislation in the (New) European Union: A Constitutional Analysis', *Modern Law Review* 74.5 (2011).

80   See also Bast, 'New Categories of Acts', n. 77: 'In terms of phenomenology, they (i.e. delegated acts, TvdB) closely resemble earlier implementing acts.'

81   P.P. Craig, 'Delegated Acts, Implementing Acts and the New Comitology Regulation', *European Law Review* 36 (2011).

82   C-427/12, Case C-88/14.

83   Case C-427/12.

In other words, the formal criteria for the application of Articles 290 and 291 TFEU must be complied with, but within that framework the EU legislature enjoys freedom and the ECJ provides no dividing line or criteria to distinguish delegation and implementation in an objective manner.[84] Also, the question whether the Commission has been granted a discretionary power or not (or if so, the scope thereof) is not a relevant factor to determine whether Article 290 or 291 should apply. Many issues on how delegated acts and implementing acts should be applied are thus left open.[85]

The distinction between delegation and implementation is in the hands of the EU legislature and has in practice become extremely politicized. This had resulted in considerable delays in legislative processes, including in major legislative dossiers such as the Multiannual Financial Framework, the reform of the Common Agricultural Policy and the series of measures relating to the Single Market Act I (April 2011) and II (October 2012).[86] The Member States in the Council usually favour either regulating as much as possible by legislative acts or leaving matters to be further regulated by implementing acts.[87] By contrast, the European Parliament usually favours delegation because of the stronger powers of control,[88] which it lacks under Article 291 TFEU.[89] The Commission promised already in 2009 to 'systematically consult experts from the national authorities of all the Member States'[90] – and this commitment has indeed been incorporated

---

84   D. Ritleng, 'The Dividing Line between Delegated and Implementing Acts: The Court of Justice Sidesteps the Difficulty in *Commission v Parliaments and Council (Biocides)*', *Common Market Law Review* 52.1 (2014).

85   A. Héritier, C. Moury, 'The Contest for Power in Delegated Rulemaking', in C.F. Bergström, D. Ritleng (eds), *Rulemaking by the EU Commission: The New System of Delegation of Powers* (Oxford: Oxford Scholarship Online, 2016).

86   For the details, see: http://ec.europa.eu/growth/single-market/smact/index_nl.htm.

87   Christiansen and Dobbels, 'Non-Legislative Rule Making'.

88   A way out has been found by creating a semi-new legal act: the 'amending delegated act': Héritier and Moury, 'The Contest for Power'.

89   Article 11 of the Comitology Regulation (Regulation 182/2011/EU laying down the rules and general principles concerning mechanisms for control by Member States of the Commission's exercise of implementing powers) does provide for a mechanism of scrutiny of implementing acts for the Council and the European Parliament: if either of these institutions indicates that a draft implementing act exceeds the implementing powers of the Commission provided for in the basic act, the Commission needs to review. However, as Craig has noted, the limits of this mechanisms are notable, and do not extend to the Commission having to withdraw or amend an implementing act to which the Council or the European Parliament have objected (Craig, 'Delegated Acts').

90   Communication of the Commission to the European Parliament and the Council of 9 December 2009, COM(2009) 673 final.

into various legislative acts[91] – to take away Member States' opposition against delegation.

This has been formalized in the 2016 Interinstitutional Agreement on Better Law-Making (IIA):[92]

- It is now an obligation for the Commission to consult Member State experts
- The Commission is obliged to react to the consultation of Member State experts and will state how it will take the experts' views into consideration
- Member State experts have the right to give a new opinion in case of a change in the material content of a draft delegated act.

In its proposal for the IIA, the Commission had proposed to identify a set of objective criteria to guide the choice between delegation and implementation.[93] The proposal included a number of criteria that in fact directly flow from the Treaty system, such as the rule that measures designed to lay down additional substantive rules and criteria to be met can only be adopted by way of delegated acts as they supplement the basic act.[94] Other criteria would have been new, such as the principle that the 'Annual and multiannual work programmes implementing financial instruments should be adopted by means of implementing acts'.[95] Even a vague commitment to negotiate substantive criteria between the three institutions following the entry into force of the IIA has not made it to the final text.[96] The choice between delegation and implementation will thus remain an issue of ad hoc political choice.

---

91   For example, in the field of pensions in Directive 2013/14/EU (institutions for occupational retirement provision, undertakings for collective investment in transferable securities and managers of alternative investment funds). Recital 3 of the directive provides: 'It is of particular importance that the Commission carry out appropriate consultations during its preparatory work, including at expert level, and that it publish the results of such consultations.'
92   Interinstitutional Agreement between the European Parliament, the Council of the European Union and the European Commission on Better Law-Making of 12 May 2016, OJ L 123.
93   COM(2015) 216 final.
94   Consideration 8, Common Understanding between the European Parliament, the Council and the Commission on Delegated Acts, Annex I to the Commission's Proposal, COM(2015) 216 final.
95   Idem, consideration 14.
96   Common Understanding on Delegated Acts, which is part of the above-mentioned IIA.

2.5   Rule-making and EU agencies

A last issue is the role of EU agencies in rule-making. Both the treaties and the IIA completely ignore the issue.[97] Nevertheless, the EU financial agencies that have been set up in 2011, including EIOPA (European Insurance and Occupational Pensions Authority), have been granted quasi-regulatory powers and are authorized to propose draft delegated and implementing acts. The status of such draft acts is strengthened by legislative constraints on the discretion of the Commission. The Commission may not simply ignore such draft acts. Thus, the existence of such quasi-regulatory powers raises questions as to their exact status and scope, their legitimacy and the implications to the EU institutions. In any case, the decision of the ECJ in ESMA (discussed above) confirms that the existence of such quasi-delegating and quasi-implementing powers are not per se unconstitutional.

---

97   H.C.H. Hofmann, 'Legislation, Delegation and Implementation under the Treaty of Lisbon: Typology Meets Reality', *European Law Journal* 15.4 (2009).

3   Occupational pensions and the freedom to provide services[1]

3.1   Introduction

The previous chapters made apparent that pension policy is not exclusively a national competence. Chapter 2 shed light on some of the EU's competences in the pension field, and also made clear that Member States' pension systems affect the EU's internal market. Therefore – though the responsibility of regulating pension systems rests primarily with the Member States – those national pension systems must not unduly interfere with the functioning of the Single Market. The obligation for national pension systems to respect the requirements of the Single Market shall be explained by way of the example of compulsory membership in occupational pensions in relation to the freedom to provide services – a fundamental EU law principle aiming at ensuring the free movement of services throughout the territory of the EU.

The rationale for making membership in an occupational pension scheme compulsory is manifold. First, compulsory retirement saving can protect individuals against their own myopia: it is often difficult to foresee one's own needs in retirement, and the absence of an obligation to save could lead to insufficient preparation.[2] In addition, compulsory membership can lead to cost savings created by the economies of scale resulting from a large number of pension scheme participants obliged to join the scheme.[3] A large membership base also allows for the sharing of risks through solidarity within pension schemes. Such solidarity can manifest itself in, for instance, 'the obligation to accept all workers without a prior medical examination, the continuing accrual of pension rights despite exemption from contributions in the event of incapacity for work, the discharge of the fund of arrears of contributions due from an employer in the event of the latter's insolvency and by the indexing of the amount of the pensions in order to maintain their

---

1   Parts of this chapter appeared in: H. van Meerten, E.S. Schmidt, 'Compulsory Membership of Pension Schemes and the Free Movement of Services in the EU', *European Journal of Social Security* 19.2 (2017).
2   S. Hoff, *Pensioenen: solidariteit en keuzevrijheid: Opvattingen van werkenden over aanvullende pensioenen* (The Hague: Sociaal en Cultureel Planbureau, 2015).
3   D. Chen, R. Beetsma, 'Mandatory Participation in Occupational Pension Schemes in the Netherlands and Other Countries: An Update', Netspar Academic Series Paper (2015).

value' as well as an 'absence of any equivalence, for individuals, between the contribution paid [...] and pension rights'.[4] The European Court of Justice recognized the importance of compulsory membership for the organization of solidarity where it noted that compulsory affiliation is 'indispensable for application of the principle of solidarity and the financial equilibrium of those schemes'.[5] It has also recognized the 'special nature' of occupational pensions that are based on mandatory collective agreements.[6]

In the Netherlands, the country with the highest pension assets to GDP ratio in the world,[7] compulsory membership in sectoral pension schemes has contributed significantly to the approximately €1700 billion of accumulated pension assets.[8] The Dutch rationale for making participation in a sectoral pension fund mandatory is twofold, according to the explanatory memorandum to the Dutch Pensions Act. First, its aim is to eliminate competition between employers in respect of the pension arrangements that they offer their employees. This supposedly prevents a race to the bottom in terms of employment conditions.[9] Second, there is a social goal in ensuring that all employees within a certain sector have identical pension arrangements so as to protect weaker workers,[10] adding a solidarity element.[11] For these reasons, compulsory membership is valued highly by, for example, the Dutch government.[12]

Although compulsory membership in occupational pensions therefore certainly seems to have its merits, the systems underpinning such compulsion must not come into conflict with EU law. It seems that compulsory affiliation to one – or a limited number – of providers – limiting or abrogating entirely the possibility for an employee or employer to choose – does just that. The obligation for pension scheme participants to be affiliated to one particular provider appears to necessarily limit both components of the freedom to provide services.[13] On the one hand is the possibility for pension

---

4   Case C-67/96.
5   Joined Cases C-159/91 and C-160/91.
6   W. Baugniet, *The Protection of Occupational Pensions under European Union Law on the Freedom of Movement for Workers*, PhD diss., European University Institute, 2014.
7   This rate stands at 193.8%. See Willis Towers Watson, *Global Pension Assets Study* (2018).
8   CBS, 'Nationaal vermogen gestegen door grotere pensioenpot', 24 February 2016.
9   M. Heemskerk, *Pensioenrecht* (The Hague: Boom Juridische Uitgevers, 2015).
10   Ibid.
11   E. Schols-van Oppen, *Inleiding pensioenrecht* (Deventer: Wolters Kluwer, 2015).
12   M. van der Poel, *De houdbaarheid van verplicht gestelde bedrijfstakpensioenfondsen en beroepspensioenregelingen: Toetsing aan het mededingingsrecht en het vrij verkeer van diensten en vestiging* (Amsterdam: Expertisecentrum Pensioenrecht Vrije Universiteit Amsterdam, 2013).
13   Cases 286/82 and 26/83.

providers to offer pension schemes in a Member State with compulsory membership. On the other hand, compulsory membership also deprives employers and/or employees to pick a pension provider of their own choosing. Such restrictions can, under certain circumstances, be justified.

Compulsory membership in a certain pension scheme, while the choice of provider remains free, seems unproblematic from the perspective of the freedom to provide services.

This chapter explains, first, the relationship between compulsory membership and European law and jurisprudence from the European Court of Justice (ECJ or the Court). It will then study how compulsory membership is organized in the Netherlands and a selection of other EU countries and will assess those systems of (quasi-) mandatory participation from the perspective of European law and the ECJ's case law. Because of the size of the Dutch schemes, some extra attention will be paid to the Netherlands.

The main question that is addressed in this chapter is: Can a justification be found in EU law for mandatory participation in a pension fund and/or in a pension scheme?

3.2 Compulsory membership and the freedom to provide services

Article 56 TFEU guarantees the freedom to provide services and is one of the cornerstones of the EU's Single Market. The article contains a prohibition against any restriction of the freedom to provide services,[14] and the Court has made clear in its jurisprudence that any form of discrimination against the service provider on the ground of nationality as well as any other barriers restricting the provision of services is contrary to the freedom enshrined in the article.[15] Even minor restrictions are prohibited.[16]

The freedom to provide services can be restricted in three main ways: by directly discriminatory measures, indirectly discriminatory measures and measures that are neither directly nor indirectly discriminatory. Direct discrimination arises when persons, goods or services from other Member States are treated differently than nationals strictly on account of their

---

14 D. Chalmers, G. Davies, G. Monti, *European Union Law: Text and Materials*, 3rd ed. (Cambridge: Cambridge University Press, 2014).

15 Case C-76/90.

16 Case C-49/89

nationality.[17] Indirect discrimination occurs when the difference in treatment does not appear to be based on nationality, but ultimately has the effect of disadvantaging persons, goods or services from other Member States. The third category of measures is broader than the previous two, and was explained by the Court in *Säger*: it ruled that Article 56 TFEU requires the elimination

> of any restriction, even if it applies without distinction to national providers of services and to those of other Member States, when it is liable to prohibit or otherwise impede the activities of a provider of services established in another Member State where he lawfully provides similar services.[18]

3.2.1   Compulsory membership: An obstacle to the freedom to provide services?

Compulsory membership in occupational pension schemes can take a number of forms. First, there can be a statutory obligation for the employer and/or employee to contribute to a particular pension scheme or pension account. Such an obligation can either leave the choice of the provider up to the individual or employer, or prescribe a particular provider. Another way of organizing compulsory membership is the obligation arising out of a collective labour agreement, the application of which can – in some EU Member States[19] – be extended to all employees within a particular sector. That collective agreement can appoint a particular scheme or a particular pension provider to which affiliation becomes mandatory for employees and/or employers.

Which of these forms could be problematic from the perspective of EU law? In *Kattner Stahlbau*,[20] a case concerning mandatory insurance against accidents at work and occupational diseases, the Court assessed the existence of an obstacle as follows. The Court held that

> [i]t must accordingly be ascertained, first, whether it restricts the ability of insurance companies established in other Member States to offer their insurance services relating to some or all of the risks in question on the market

---

17   See Case C-288/89, para. 10.
18   Case C-76/90, para. 12.
19   See para. 3.3.
20   Case C-350/07.

of the first Member State and, second, whether it discourages undertakings established in that first Member State, in their capacity as recipients of services, from taking out insurance with those insurance companies.[21]

Although *Kattner Stahlbau* does not concern occupational pensions, it is nonetheless relevant for its considerations on the compulsory element of the insurance scheme at issue in that case. After reiterating that the freedom to provide services requires the elimination of all discrimination on the grounds of nationality and other restrictions that may prohibit, impede or render less advantageous the provision of services,[22] the Court ruled that the system of compulsory membership caused a restriction of the freedom to provide services for companies in other Member States.[23] Such restrictions must be justified, for instance on the grounds that the financial equilibrium of the pension system could be jeopardized.[24]

Based on the foregoing it appears that all forms of compulsory membership in one or a limited number of pension providers limit the freedom to provide services to some degree: individual employers and/or employees cannot choose a pension provider of their own preference and, likewise, those prospective providers are unable to offer their services to employers and employees bound by compulsory membership. In particular, a system of compulsory membership that prescribes affiliation to one particular national provider, such as that in place in the Netherlands, seems especially problematic, as will be demonstrated below. A system that pre-selects a limited number of providers, such as the one in place in Sweden, also seems to be an obstacle to the freedom to provide services (however that obstacle could potentially be justified), as there does not appear to be a bar on non-Swedish providers and – therefore – no direct discrimination. Possible justifications for such obstacles will be discussed in the next section.

3.2.2 Justifying obstacles to the freedom to provide services

In principle the treaty takes precedence over the IORP II Directive.[25] IORP II regulates, inter alia, the cross-border activities of so-called IORPs

---

21 Ibid., para. 77.
22 Ibid., para. 78.
23 Ibid., para. 82.
24 Ibid., paras 85 et seq.
25 Directive 2016/2341/EU of the European Parliament and of the Council of 14 December 2016 on the activities and supervision of institutions for occupational retirement provision (IORPs). See Craig and De Búrca, *EU Law*.

(institutions for occupational retirement provision). Like the treaty, IORP II also contains provisions that are relevant to the free movement of services in relation to compulsory membership. Preamble 22 of IORP II proclaims that

> Without prejudice to national social and labour legislation on the organization of pension systems, *including compulsory membership* and the outcomes of collective bargaining agreements, IORPs should have the possibility of providing their services in other Member States upon receipt of the authorization from the competent authority of the IORP's home Member State [italics added].

The IORP II Directive provides an express exception for systems of compulsory membership and collective bargaining. However, it will be demonstrated that this exception should not be taken to mean that simply any system of compulsory membership is acceptable under the freedom to provide services. Compulsory membership in occupational pensions was subject to the ECJ's scrutiny in a number of cases, albeit mainly from the perspective of competition law and not the freedom to provide services. The Court reasoned in *Albany*, a case concerning a Dutch mandatory sectoral pension scheme, that the collective agreement making affiliation to a pension scheme mandatory falls outside the ambit of competition law. As a consequence, so does the decision by public authorities to make affiliation to a sectoral pension fund compulsory. The Court decided also that, while indeed granting an exclusive right to the fund at issue constituted a violation of the competition rules, such a violation was justified due to the essential social function that the fund fulfils.

Thanks to the qualification by the ECJ of the services offered by the pension provider in *Albany* as services of general economic interest (SGEI), the mandatory pension scheme at issue in *Albany* was able to benefit from the exception in Article 106(2) TFEU. The article provides that undertakings entrusted with services of general economic interest are subject to the rules on 'in particular' competition, unless the application of those hampers the performance of the tasks assigned to them. However, the fact that a certain agreement or action – in this case the request to make membership in a sectoral pension fund mandatory, the government act making such a decision as well as the conduct of the sectoral pension funds – would be acceptable under the provisions of competition law does not mean that such matters are equally allowed under the freedom-of-movement provisions.[26]

26   H. van Meerten 'Vrij verkeer van diensten voor verzekeraars en pensioeninstellingen: Solvency II basic en de verplichtstelling', *Tijdschrift voor financieel recht* 7/8 (2012).

The ECJ has decided to this effect in, for instance, *Commission v Germany*[27] and *Viking*[28] – contrary to the Dutch Supreme Court.[29]

The ECJ has developed a number of criteria in its case law that may justify non-discriminatory restrictions on the free movement clauses in the treaty.[30] In *Gebhard*,[31] the Court ruled that

> national measures liable to hinder or make less attractive the exercise of fundamental freedoms guaranteed by the Treaty must fulfil four conditions: they must be applied in a non-discriminatory manner; they must be justified by imperative requirements in the general interest; they must be suitable for securing the attainment of the objective which they pursue; and they must not go beyond what is necessary in order to attain it.

In principle, measures concerning direct discrimination – such as a distinction on grounds of nationality – may only be justified using the exceptions enumerated in Article 52 TFEU.[32] These grounds are public policy, public security and public health. The grounds for justification of restrictions that apply without discrimination differ from those that apply with discrimination,[33] although it is sometimes difficult to tell the difference.[34] Generally speaking, it can be said that a breach of discriminatory measures is harder to justify than a breach of a non-discriminatory clause.[35]

On the other hand, because of the phrase 'in particular the rules on competition'[36] used in Article 106(2) TFEU, there is an 'outspread assumption' that the article can also be used to justify an exemption for,

---

27 Case C-271/08.

28 Case C-438/05.

29 Van der Poel, *De houdbaarheid*.

30 T. Kennedy, *European Law* (Oxford: Oxford University Press, 2011).

31 Case C-55/94.

32 M. Wiberg, *The EU Services Directive: Law or Simply Policy?* (Amsterdam: TMC Asser Press, 2014).

33 Case C-388/01.

34 J. van der Beek, 'Een vrijkaartje voor EG-65-plussers bij alle Italiaanse musea', *Nederlands tijdschrift voor Europees recht* 6 (2003).

35 Ibid.

36 The full text of Article 106(2) TFEU reads as follows: 'Undertakings entrusted with the operation of services of general economic interest or having the character of a revenue-producing monopoly shall be subject to the rules contained in the treaties, in particular to the rules on competition, in so far as the application of such rules does not obstruct the performance, in law or in fact, of the particular tasks assigned to them. The development of trade must not be affected to such an extent as would be contrary to the interests of the Union.'

inter alia, the free movement rules.[37] Unfortunately, the ECJ has thus far left unused an invitation to clarify the relationship between the exception of Article 106(2) TFEU and Article 56 TFEU. Those who support this opinion[38] proffer the idea that the justifications used in *Albany* under the competition rules can be used also to justify obstacles to the freedom to provide services.

Let us now return to *Kattner Stahlbau*,[39] the case discussed in the previous section concerning mandatory insurance against accidents at work and occupational diseases. The Court found that the system at issue in this case may constitute a restriction of the freedom to provide services, as it 'hinders or renders less attractive, or even prevents, directly or indirectly, the exercise of that freedom'[40] both for insurance companies established in other Member States to offer their services in the Member State concerned, as well as the freedom of businesses that are affected to select a provider from abroad. The ECJ said that although the regulation of social security matters is a prerogative of the Member States, that prerogative must be exercised in accordance with the freedom to provide services. In particular, this means that the freedoms afforded by the treaties under the freedom to provide services must be adhered to.

The ECJ finds, however, that a restriction to the freedom of services may be justified by overriding requirements relating to the public interest. Such restrictions must be in accordance with the proportionality principle and must be suitable to attain the objective pursued. In particular, the Court recognized the importance of safeguarding the financial equilibrium of the system at issue.[41] It stressed that compulsory membership was necessary to enable the scheme to apply the principle of solidarity, which in that case was 'characterised, in particular, by funding through contributions the amount of which is not strictly proportionate to the risks insured and by the granting of benefits the amount of which is not strictly proportionate to contributions'.[42] Although that case concerned mandatory insurance

---

37   U. Neergaard, 'The Concept of SSGI and the Asymmetries Between Free Movement and Competition Law', in U. Neergaard, et al. (eds), *Social Services of General Interest in the EU* (The Hague: T.M.C. Asser Press, 2013).

38   B. Drijber, 'Modernisering van het Uitvoeringsmodel voor Pensioenregelingen: Grenzen en mogelijkheden vanuit mededingingsrechtelijk en Europeesrechtelijk perspectief', Report for the Ministry of Social Affairs and Employment, 22 March 2007.

39   Case C-350/07.

40   Ibid.

41   Ibid, paras 85-88.

42   Ibid., para. 87.

against accidents at work and occupational diseases, the arguments could have some bearing on occupational pensions.

Although the solidarity of the scheme played an important role, the existence of such solidarity is not an automatic justification to apply restrictions to the freedom to provide services. In *Commission v Germany*, the Court noted that elements of solidarity are 'not inherently irreconcilable' with the application of a procurement procedure.[43]

Although the restrictive character of compulsory membership on the freedom to provide services can under certain circumstances be justified, it is important to stress that (1) different justifications are available depending on the nature of the restriction and (2) the restriction must be proportional. Given the more limited possibilities for the justification of directly discriminatory obstacles for the freedom to provide services, it seems clear that a system of compulsory membership that excludes providers from other Member States a priori will be difficult to justify. This seems all the more true given the fact that such justifications must pass a proportionality test. Compulsory membership in a national fund – by law and under certain circumstances by a decision by social partners – appears to be an obstacle to the freedom to provide services that is directly discriminatory, and can in principle be justified only by the exceptions contained in Article 52 TFEU. IORPs from other Member States would no longer be able to offer their services in the state that has made affiliation to a domestic fund compulsory.

To summarize the preceding paragraphs of this section, restrictions of the freedom to provide services can be permissible in principle. However, a distinction must be made between discriminatory restrictions and non-discriminatory restrictions.[44] Discriminatory restrictions on the freedom to provide services (for instance, if national pension funds are treated more favourably than providers from another Member State) can be justified in principle only on the grounds mentioned in Article 52 TFEU. Non-discriminatory measures

> must be applied in a non-discriminatory manner; they must be justified by overriding reasons based on the general interest; they must be suitable for securing the attainment of the objective which they pursue; and they must not go beyond what is necessary in order to attain that objective.[45]

---

43 Case C-271/08.

44 H. van Meerten, 'Directe horizontale werking van het vrije dienstenverkeer', in Bastiaan Starink, Michael Visser (eds), *Ondernemend met pensioen* (Deventer: Wolters Kluwer, 2015).

45 Case C-294/00.

3.2.3   The UNIS case

What is more, the Court ruled that when public authorities exercise an exclusive right – such as a ministerial decision to extend the application of a collective agreement to appoint a single body for the administration of an insurance or pension scheme – the principle of transparency must be complied with.[46] This principle stems from the principles of equal treatment and non-discrimination. According to the ECJ in *UNIS*, the principle does not necessarily require a public call for tenders, but it does require 'a degree of publicity sufficient to enable, on the one hand, competition to be opened up and, on the other, the impartiality of the award procedure to be reviewed'.[47] So, while Member States may create exclusive rights for certain service providers, the principle of transparency must be complied with.

In a similar vein, the social partners must abide by the same requirements mentioned in the preceding paragraphs when selecting a pension provider. The ECJ pointed out in *Viking* that it is settled case law that the requirements on the fundamental freedoms apply not only 'to the actions of public authorities but extend also to rules of any other nature aimed at regulating in a collective manner gainful employment, self-employment and the provision of services'.[48] The social partners are, therefore, obliged to take into account the same requirements as public authorities. This, taken together with the ECJ's decision in *UNIS*, means that the principle of transparency, stemming from the principles of equal treatment and non-discrimination that must be observed in the context of Article 56 TFEU, must also be complied with by the social partners.

For these reasons, too, the fact that the IORP II Directive contains the phrase '[w]ithout prejudice to national social and labor law [...], including compulsory membership' with respect to cross-border activity cannot lead to a conclusion that Article 12 of the IORP II Directive allows for the exclusion of pension providers from other Member States for the operation of mandatory sectoral pension schemes.[49]

---

46   Joined Cases C-25/14 and C-26/14.
47   Ibid., para. 39.
48   Case C-438/05.
49   Lutjens, for example, states – without giving further reasons – that this phrase allows for the exclusion of foreign provides. See: E. Lutjens, *Bijzondere overeenkomsten: Pensioen* (Deventer: Wolters Kluwer, 2016).

3.3   Comparison: Mandatory participation in a selection of Member States

Now that the applicable legislation and case law has been studied in detail, it will be examined how systems of mandatory participation have been organized in a selection of Member States and whether these feature a system that excludes providers from other Member States. The countries studied below feature two separate models when it comes to mandatory participation. In Denmark and Sweden, collective agreements regulate most of the areas of labour law and largely substitute for statutory legislation and apply to all employees in a particular sector without government intervention.[50] In Germany, France, Belgium and the Netherlands, a government act is required to extend the application of collective agreements. In either case, it is clear that the case law described in this contribution, and the requirements of the freedom to provide services as well as the principle of transparency, applies to both models.

3.3.1   Compulsory membership in the Netherlands

Compulsory membership of sectoral pension funds in the Netherlands is currently regulated by the Act on Compulsory Membership of a Sectoral Pension Fund 2000 (Bpf Act). Occupational pensions in the Netherlands are quasi-mandatory. This means that, while in principle there is no statutory obligation for all employed persons to be affiliated to an occupational (second pillar) pension scheme, participation in such schemes is near-universal at more than 90% of Dutch employees.[51] In addition to the Bpf Act is the Wet verplichte beroepspensioenregeling (Mandatory Professional Pension Scheme Act, or Wvb). The Wvb concerns professions rather than the industry sectors to which the Bpf Act applies. These professions include dentistry, veterinary medicine, physiotherapy, medical specialists, midwives, maritime pilots, independent artists etc.[52]

---

50   O. Hasselbach, *Labour Law in Denmark* (Alphen a/d Rijn: Kluwer Law International/DJØF, 2010), p. 40; A. Adlercreutz and B. Nyström, *Labor Law in Sweden* (Alphen a/d Rijn: Kluwer Law International, 2010).

51   Chen and Beetsma, 'Mandatory Participation'.

52   S. Kuiper, 'De bevoegdheden van werkgevers en werknemers om een pensioenuitvoerder te kiezen: zeggenschap in het Nederlandse pensioenstelsel', AIAS Working Paper, Amsterdam Institute for Advanced Labour Studies, 2013.

3.3.1.1 The Bpf Act and the Wvb

The Bpf Act empowers the Dutch minister of social affairs and employment to make participation in a sectoral pension fund (known in the Netherlands as a *bedrijfstakpensioenfonds*, or Bpf) of a particular sector of industry mandatory at the request of a 'significant majority' of social partners in that sector.[53] The consequence of the minister's decision to make participation mandatory is that in principle all those who fall within its scope must participate in the sectoral pension fund. This mechanism can also be found in Belgium, France and Germany. It applies to employers as well as employees, regardless of whether or not they are organized in a trade union or employers' association, and whether they want to participate or not. Because of this policy, over 75% of Dutch employees who have some type of pension arrangement participate in a mandatory sectoral pension scheme.[54]

Crucially, from the perspective of the freedom to provide services, mandatory sectoral pension schemes may be operated only by a *pensioenfonds*, a Dutch pension fund. This arises out of the definition of what a sectoral pension fund is under the Dutch Pensions Act, to which the Bpf Act refers. The Pensions Act distinguishes between a 'pension fund' and a 'pension institution'. It defines a sectoral pension fund as a *pensioenfonds*. A *pensioenfonds*, in turn, is defined as; 'a foundation [*stichting*] which is not a premium pension institution (PPI)'.[55] A Bpf, therefore, is to be erected according to the legal form stichting, a Dutch foundation, thereby excluding non-Dutch providers. Based on these definitions, membership cannot be made compulsory to a non-Dutch pension provider, and this has indeed been affirmed by the minister of social affairs and employment.[56]

The Wvb works in a manner similar to the Bpf Act. The important difference between the two acts is that in the Wvb it the scheme rather than the fund to which affiliation is made mandatory by the minister.[57] The choice of pension provider under the Wvb seems to be left open for the profession's association (the pension association) responsible for organizing

---

53 Article 2 of Act on Compulsory Membership of a Sector Pension Fund 2000. In order for the majority to be deemed significant, the number of employees working at the requesting businesses must represent at least 60% of the total number of workers employed within the sector. Under certain conditions, a lower ratio may be classified as significant, but any percentage under 50% cannot yield a significant majority under any circumstances.

54 Kuiper (2013).

55 Article 1 of the Dutch Pensions Act.

56 Kamerstukken II 2006/07, 28 294, 29.

57 Article 5 of the Mandatory Professional Pension Schemes Act.

the pension scheme, the *beroepspensioenvereniging*. The scheme can in principle therefore be operated by one of the three categories of Dutch pension providers – pension funds, insurance companies and premium pension institutions (PPIs)[58] – or a pension provider from another Member State.[59]

Given this availability to choose for a provider from another Member State, the Wvb appears to be, in principle, no obstacle to the free movement of services. However, there is a caveat. Under the Wvb the administration of the mandatory scheme may be operated only by one provider for the entire profession. This provider is chosen by the pension association. In this respect, the freedom of choice under this type of mandatory participation also appears limited.

The social partners in the Netherlands design the scheme and its features in collective labour agreements. The minister of social affairs and employment can, at the request of a 'significant majority' of a particular sector of industry, make participation in the occupational pension scheme mandatory by extending the application of the collective agreement to all parties defined in it. In the Netherlands, only Dutch *pensioenfondsen*, which must have the legal form of a *stichting* (i.e. a foundation), may operate a mandatory sectoral scheme. Non-Dutch pension providers are therefore excluded from operating mandatory sectoral pension schemes. It is this requirement which is the main focus of this article.

3.3.1.2 Compulsory membership in the Netherlands: Direct discrimination
According to the Bpf Act's explanatory memorandum, the existence of mandatory participation is justified by the social end that these sectoral pension funds pursue; they feature a high degree of solidarity between a variety of cohorts.[60] Indeed, according to the ECJ this social goal is what justifies mandatory participation, which inherently distorts competition, from the perspective of competition law.[61] But considering the preceding paragraphs, it seems that the manner in which mandatory participation is arranged in the Netherlands could not survive a test against the freedom to

---

58 H. van Meerten, 'De premiepensioenstelling: van, maar ook op vele markten thuis?', *Nederlands tijdschrift voor Europees recht* 12 (2008).

59 Article 8 of the Mandatory Professional Pension Schemes Act; see: H. van Meerten, H. van den Hout, 'De pensioenaanbieder: nationaal en internationaal', in E. Lutjens (ed.), *Pensioenwet: Analyse en commentaar* (Deventer: Kluwer, 2013).

60 Explanatory Memorandum to the Sectoral Pension Funds Act 2000, Kamerstukken II 2000/01, 27 073, 3.

61 C-67/96, para. 59.

provide services. It excludes directly non-Dutch providers from the market for mandatory occupational pensions. The only justificatory grounds for such direct discrimination are those enumerated in Article 52 TFEU: public policy, public security and public health. Even though the Court has 'occasionally' accepted objective justifications in the case of directly discriminatory measures, these measures still need to pass a proportionality test. It seems rather unlikely that an absolute exclusion by law of providers from other Member States could withstand such a test, certainly in light of the above-mentioned case law. With respect to the current system of mandatory participation in the Netherlands, there appears to be no valid reason why the provider for mandatory sectoral pension schemes must be a Dutch *pensioenfonds*.

A change in the manner in which compulsory membership is organized in the Netherlands could bring the necessary change to bring the Dutch system in line with European law. The first, and most obvious change in that context, would appear to be to let go of the requirement that the provider for a compulsory sectoral scheme must be Dutch. Another solution would be to change the compulsory element by not making participation in a particular fund mandatory, but the scheme, while allowing social partners to select a provider from any Member States.[62]

3.3.2   Sweden

Occupational pensions in Sweden are, as in the Netherlands, quasi-mandatory through collective bargaining. What is different about Sweden (and Denmark) is that there is no possibility for government intervention to make collective agreements generally binding.[63] The country's 'robust collective bargaining system with mandatory occupational pension coverage' is the foundation of occupational pensions in Sweden.[64]

About 90% of Swedish employees is covered by an occupational pension scheme.[65] There are four main schemes in Sweden, with a number of additional schemes covering smaller sectors.[66] The four main schemes

---

62   P. Borsjé, 'Verplichtstelling aan de regeling: serieus alternatief?', *Pensioen Advies* 1/2, februari 2016.

63   G. Sebardt, 'Last in, First out? The Agency Work Directive and the Swedish Staffing Industry as Part of the Swedish Labour-Market Model', in Jens Kristiansen (ed.), *Europe and the Nordic Collective-Bargaining Model: The Complex Interaction between Nordic and European Labour Law* (Copenhagen: Nordic Council of Ministers, 2015).

64   K.M. Anderson, 'Occupational Pensions in Sweden', Friedrich Ebert Stiftung, December 2015.

65   Ibid.

66   N. Barr, *The Pension System in Sweden* (Stockholm: Elanders Sverige AB, 2013).

are: (1) the SAF-LO scheme for blue-collar workers, (2) the ITP scheme for white-collar workers, (3) the PA 03 scheme for central government employees and (4) the KAP-KL scheme for county council and municipal employees. Each of the collective agreements is managed by an administrative body that collects the pension contributions paid by the employees and employers, and redirects the funds to the insurance company chosen by the employee.[67] The administrative bodies managing the schemes also select a number of insurance companies from which the employee can then choose. These administrative bodies, in turn, are managed by the social partners, who select and negotiate the conditions for the providers of pension services.

Because Sweden's quasi-mandatory occupational pension system is based mainly on collective agreements, there appears to be no formal legislation setting any requirements as to the nationality of the provider.

3.3.3   Denmark

The system for collective bargaining in Denmark is highly regulated, but not by formal legislation as in, for example, the Netherlands. The Danish regulation is the consequence of the September Compromise of 1899, in which employers' associations recognized the fact that workers have the right to organize in trade unions and, vice versa, these trade unions accepted the right to management of the employers. The September Compromise is still considered to be at the base of the Danish labour market today, 'where the vast majority of employment terms and conditions are determined by agreement between the labour market parties as opposed to statutory regulations'.[68] This means that there are relatively few statutory labour and employment rules in Denmark.[69] Those that do exist are typically the consequence of EU law.

As in the Netherlands and Sweden, Denmark's second pillar consists of quasi-mandatory occupational pension schemes that complement the flat, universal public pension.[70] In all three countries, the statutory pension is aimed at poverty relief, while the second pillar's role is to supplement

67   A.L. Bovenberg, R. Cox, S. Lundbergh, 'Lessons from the Swedish Occupational Pension System: Are Mutual Life Insurance Companies a Relevant Model for Occupational Pensions in the Netherlands', Design Paper – Netspar Industry Paper Series 45, Netspar.

68   PWC, *Labour Law in Denmark* (2009).

69   Ibid.

70   O. Beier Sørensen, C. Dengsøe, 'Elements of the Danish System Relevant to the Dutch Pension Sector', Peer Review of the Netherlands' Pension System conference, The Hague, April 2011, http://ec.europa.eu/social/BlobServlet?docId=8238&langId=en.

the basic provision and to maintain living standards proportionally. Like Sweden's system, the system for occupational pensions in Denmark was created by collective bargaining processes rather than by a legislative process.[71] There is no possibility for the government to extend application of a collective agreement.[72] Around 80% of Danish workers are members of an occupational pension scheme.[73]

The social partners determine the design and content of the pension schemes in collective agreements, and the resultant schemes are the direct results from such bargaining.[74] This means that these schemes are contractual. The social partners also decide on the company that administers the pension scheme.[75] There is no formal legislation on this subject in Denmark.[76] Given the absence of such legislation, there appears to be no obligation for the social partners to opt for a Danish provider.

3.3.4 Germany

Though the public pension system in Germany is dominant,[77] second pillar arrangements are becoming more prevalent as trust in the public scheme wanes[78] and public benefits were cut in recent reforms.[79] The importance of such schemes for future retirement incomes is also on the

71   J. Hansen, S. Hougaard Jensen, P. Sephensen, 'Occupational Pensions, Aggregate Saving and Fiscal Sustainability in Denmark', Taking the Danish Pension System to the Next Stage: PeRCent's First Annual Conference, Copenhagen, June 2015.

72   N. Bruun, 'The *Vaxholm* Case and Its "Solidarity Lessons" from a Swedish and European Perspective', in L. Magnusson, B. Stråth (eds), *European Solidarities: Tensions and Contentions of a Concept* (Brussels: P.I.E. Peter Lang SA, 2007).

73   Centraal Planbureau, 'Internationale vergelijking van pensioenstelsels: Denemakren, Zweden, Chili en Australië', 12 June 2015, https://www.cpb.nl/sites/default/files/publicaties/download/cpb-notitie-12juni2015-internationale-vergelijking-van-pensioenstelsels-denemarken-zweden-chili-aust.pdf, p. 14.

74   H. Thode, 'Ændringer i arbejdsmarkedspensionen – hvem bestemmer hvad der sker' *Nordisk Forsikringstidsskrift* (2010).

75   Pensam, 'Hvem bestemmer hvad omkring pensionen?', https://www.pensam.dk/pension/PDFfiler/Andet/Hvem%20bestemmer.pdf.

76   Ibid.

77   F. Hufeld, 'Keynote speech', OECD/IOPS Global Forum on Pensions: Pension Reform in Germany and Key Supervisory Challenges, Berlin, 29 October 2015, https://www.oecd.org/daf/fin/private-pensions/OECD-IOPS_Global-Forum_Keynote-Speech_Felix-Hufeld.pdf.

78   A. Ettel, H. Zschäpitz, 'So schlimm steht es wirklich um die deutsche Rente', *Die Welt*, 30 March (2016).

79   T. Wiß, 'From Welfare States to Welfare Sectors: Explaining Sectoral Differences in Occupational Pensions with Economic and Political Power of Employees', *Journal of European Social Policy* 25.5 (2015).

rise.[80] Germany features some occupational schemes that have been made mandatory by collective agreements. Although not nearly as prevalent as in the other countries under review in this contribution, the coverage rate of occupational pensions in Germany has increased significantly between 2001 and 2011. The percentage of private enterprises that offer occupational pension plans has grown from 31% to 50%.[81] However, this growth has slowed since 2009. Germany has implemented reforms making previously disallowed-by-law pure DC plans possible as of 1 January 2018.[82] For pure DC schemes, the proposal did away with an employer's *Subsidiärhaftung* (payment liability) enshrined in § 1(1) of the Betriebsrentengesetz (Company Pensions Act, or BetrAVG).[83]

The pension benefit obligation – the amount of money an employer must pay into the pension scheme – can arise from an individual contract, in which the employer and the employee agree to the employee's participation in a pension scheme, or from a collective agreement.[84] The agreement is binding on the parties to it without becoming a part of the employment agreement. Like in the Netherlands, and unlike in Sweden and Denmark, the Federal Ministry of Labour and Social Affairs can extend the applicability of a collective agreement to make it generally applicable.[85] The consequence of an *Allgemeinverbindlicherklärung* (extension order) is that also those employees and employers who were not parties to the agreement, will be bound to it.[86]

An aspect of German law that could be problematic from the perspective of European law is the fact that the BetrAVG allows only five types of *Durchführungswege* (implementation alternatives). These are listed in § 1(1) and represent an exhaustive list. Non-German market participants that do not match the specifications of any of the five implementation alternatives are therefore excluded from the market.

---

80 T. Wiß, *Der Wandel der Alterssicherung in Deutschland: Die Rolle der Sozialpartner* (Wiesbaden: VS Verlag für Sozialwissenschaften, 2011).

81 Bundesministerium für Arbeit und Soziales, 'Situation und Entwicklung der betrieblichen Altersversorgung in Privatwirtschaft und öffentlichem Dienst' (2012).

82 Gesetz zur Stärkung der betieblichen Altersversorgung und zur Änderung anderer Gesetze, 23.08.2017, BgBl I., 3214.

83 Ibid., Article 1.

84 F. Welker, *Das Altersvermögensgesetz und die Konsequenzen für die betriebliche Altersversorgung* (Wiesbaden: Deutscher Universitätsverlag, 2005).

85 § 5 Tarifvertragsgesetz.

86 S. Derbort et al., *Bilanzierung von Pensionsverpflichtungen: HGB, ERtG und IFRS/IAS19* (Wiesbaden: Springer Gabler, 2012).

3.3.5   Belgium

Public pensions make up roughly 80% of the retirement income for the elderly in Belgium.[87] Approximately 45% of the working-age population is covered by an occupational pension scheme.[88] Three-quarters of sectoral pension schemes are being administered by insurance companies, while eleven sectoral pension schemes are administered by IORPs. All new schemes are administered by an insurance company.[89]

Supplementary pension plans originate from collective agreements created by the social partners: the representative bodies for employers and employees who are represented in the joint committee of the sector. The social partners design the sectoral pension scheme in this joint committee,[90] which has the prerogative of implementing, altering or closing a pension scheme.[91] The collective agreement that calls the sectoral pension plan into existence must be of unlimited validity and must have been made generally applicable by the king.[92]

As in the other countries that feature a possibility to make a collective agreement generally applicable, the extension of the collective agreement has as its consequence that also those employers and employees that are not a party to the collective agreement are bound by it.[93] Any failure to comply with the obligations specified in the collective agreement is met with criminal and administrative sanctions.

The collective agreement determines the pension scheme rules.[94] It is also to indicate the choice of provider. The provider is a *pensioeninstelling*, which is defined in Article 3, § 1, 16° of the Law of 28 April 2003 on Supplementary Pensions. This provision refers to the institutions specified the Books II and III Act of 23 March 2016 relating to the statute for and supervision of insurance and reinsurance undertakings, or the institutions specified in Article 2, 1° of the Act of 26 October 2006 concerning the supervision of institutions for occupational pensions. The two books of the aforementioned act make

---

87   OECD, *Pensions at a Glance 2013: OECD and G20 Indicators* (OECD Publishing, 2013).
88   Ibid.
89   FSMA, Tweejaarlijks verslag betreffende de sectorale pensioenstelsels (April 2015).
90   Section III of the Explanatory Memorandum to the Act on Supplementary Pensions (WAP).
91   C. Hendrickx, *Uw pensioen: uw appeltje voor de dorst, ook fiscaal?* (Mechelen: Wolters Kluwer Belgium, 2013).
92   Article 10 of the Act on Supplementary Pensions (WAP).
93   Section III of the Explanatory Memorandum to the Law of 28 April 2003 on Supplementary Pensions
94   Article 8 of the Law of 28 April 2003 on Supplementary Pensions.

a distinction between insurance and reinsurance companies governed by Belgian law and foreign law. Article 2, 1° of the Act of 26 October 2006 defines a *pensioeninstelling* as an institution, regardless of legal form, that has been established for the purpose of the provision of occupational retirement benefits. It follows from this definition that there is no nationality requirement.

3.3.6 France

The French pension system is almost entirely based on a pay-as-you-go mechanism. This goes for the statutory as well as the mandatory occupational schemes.[95] The strong reliance on generous pay-as-you-go public pensions has initially crowded out funded private pensions. For many professions, the statutory scheme is complemented by a mandatory-by-law occupational scheme, such as the *régimes complémentaires obligatoires* for private sector employees. These were established by collective agreements and are managed exclusively by two federations managed by the social partners: ARRCO (Association des Régimes de Retraites Complémentaires) and AGIRC (Association Générale des Institutions de Retraites des Cadres). These federations set the rules for the pension institutions that manage the schemes.[96] Since the decision by the social partners to comply with Regulation (EEC) 1408/71, AGIRC and ARRCO schemes have been 'quasi-first pillarized'[97] and therefore do not strictly fall under the second pillar as defined by the OECD. However, cuts in these schemes started the gradual cultivation of funded private pensions.[98]

With respect to non-statutory occupational pensions, there are three main types of schemes.[99] These can all be made mandatory by a decision of the competent minister, who may extend the application of collective agreements that contain, inter alia, pension stipulations.[100] There are so-called Article 39 DB schemes and Article 83[101] DC schemes, as well as

---

95 M. Naczyk, B. Palier, 'Complementing or Replacing Old Age Insurance? The Growing Importance of Funded Pensions in the French Pension System' (2010) Working Paper REC-WP 08/2010, Reconciling Work and Welfare in Europe (2010), https://www.era.lib.ed.ac.uk/bitstream/handle/1842/3499/REC-WP_0810_Naczyk_Palier.pdf?sequence=1&isAllowed=y.

96 Ibid.

97 Ibid.

98 M. Naczyk, B. Palier, 'France: Promoting Funded Pensions in Bismarckian Corporatism?', in Bernhard Ebbinghaus (ed.), *The Varieties of Pension Governance: Pension Privatization in Europe* (Oxford: Oxford University Press, 2011).

99 Ibid.

100 Article L.911-3 of the French Social Security Code.

101 These schemes are named after the articles of the French General Code of Taxation in which they are enshrined.

PERCO.[102] Article 39 schemes 'have been generally offered to a limited
number of senior managers employed in large companies',[103] while Article 83
schemes cover a larger number of workers. Article 39 and Article 83 schemes
may be administered by insurance companies, pension funds and mutual
societies.[104]

PERCO was introduced in 2003 by the so-called 'Fillon reform' that placed
more emphasis on funded, private pensions. PERCO is an optional funded,
defined contribution scheme.[105] A PERCO scheme can be operated by a *fonds
commun de placement d'enterprise* (FCPE) or a *société d'investissement à
capital variable* (SICAV).[106] Although all three types of occupational pension
schemes are predominantly company-level schemes, they can be sector-wide.
PERCO plans are organized at firm level or by the social partners at sectoral
level,[107] while Article 39 and Article 83 plans can also be offered to only a
limited group of workers within a company.[108]

Ordonnance no. 2006-344 of 23 March 2006 has transposed the IORP
Directive into French law. Its Article 8 states that non-French IORPs can offer
their services in the field of PERCO, provided they comply with labour law
and social law applicable in France, since PERCO falls within the material
scope of the IORP Directive. According to the *ordonnance*, they benefit from
the same tax and social treatment as other PERCO providers.[109]

The *ordonnance* also applies to the occupational retirement business
of insurance companies, in particular to Articles 39 and 83 of the General
Code of Taxation, while it explicitly excludes obligatory-by-law occupational
pensions. Providers from other Member States or EEA nations may be
selected for those schemes.[110]

---

102 Y. Stevens, 'The Development of a Legal Matrix on the Meaning of "National Social and
Labour Legislation" in Directive 2003/41/EC with Regard to Five Member States', European
Association of Paritarian Institutions (AEIP), 2006.

103 Naczyk and Palier, 'France'.

104 J.-C. Naimi, 'L'IRP entrebâille la porte des fonds de pension paneuropéens', L'Agefi Actifs
(2007).

105 L. Rossi Manganotti, 'Funded Retirement Plans in France: The PERCO', *Compensation &
Benefits Review* 47.1 (2015).

106 Ibid.

107 B. Palier, 'The Dualizations of the French Welfare System', in B. Palier (ed.), *A Long Goodbye
to Bismarck?: The Politics of Welfare Reform in Continental Europe* (Amsterdam: Amsterdam
University Press, 2010).

108 Naczyk and Palier, 'Complementing or Replacing Old Age Insurance?'.

109 Rapport au Président de la République relatif à l'ordonnance n° 2006-344 du 23 mars 2006
relative aux retraites professionnelles supplémentaires (JORF du 24 mars 2006).

110 Article L. 143-4 of the Social Insurance Code.

3.4 Concluding remarks

Compulsory membership in an IORP serves a variety of important goals. In literature it is argued that it creates the large membership base required for economies of scale in the various business aspects of the pension business and the sharing of risks, known as solidarity. The obligation to contribute savings to a retirement plan also seem – according to some literature – to ensure that individuals are protected from their own short-sightedness.

However, the discussion of the relevant EU legal norms and the case law of the European Court of Justice has shown that compulsory membership constitutes an obstacle to the freedom to provide services. That obstacle can – under certain circumstances – be justified by invoking either the treaty grounds enumerated in Article 52 TFEU or, in the case of indirectly or non-discriminatory measures, the open category of objective justifications developed in the case law of the ECJ. An important argument for justifying compulsory membership could be the need to safeguard the financial equilibrium of the system at issue.

Thus far, the European Court of Justice has accepted that compulsory membership may be justified from the perspective of competition law, but has not yet specifically addressed the matter from the angle of the freedom to provide services. The social character of compulsory membership in the scheme at issue in *Albany* was cited to justify restrictions to competition. The affordability of the scheme, the absence of risk selection and various other characteristics led the ECJ to conclude that mandatory participation was allowable. Even if one were to accept that Article 106(2) TFEU can be invoked with a view to using the provision as an exemption of compulsory membership from the freedom to provide services, the party invoking the provision must still satisfy the burden of proof, also entailing a proportionality test.[111]

However, the freedom to provide services was not invoked in *Albany* and there is reason to believe that this might have led to a different outcome, given the different justifications applicable depending on the nature of the obstacle to the freedom to provide services. There appears to be no valid reason to exclude non-Dutch providers from the market to attain those goals, certainly if a foreign provider is able to offer the same pension scheme with conditions equal to or better than competing Dutch providers. The developments around the general pension fund (*algemeen pensioenfonds,*

---

111 W. Sauter, 'Services of General Economic Interest and Universal Service in EU Law', *European Law Review* 33.2 (2008).

or Apf) could have gone some way to alleviate some of the apparent discord between mandatory participation and the freedom to provide services, but for now these plans seem to be placed on hold.

For the Netherlands specifically, the high degree of solidarity – and the concomitantly delicate financial equilibrium of the schemes – would militate in favour of a justification of the breach of the freedom to provide services. However, the directly discriminatory nature of the Dutch system of compulsory membership would mean that the Court would be unlikely to accept a justification other than the ones summed up in Article 52 TFEU. Several other developments in the Netherlands may 'weaken' this solidarity, such as reduced risk sharing through the possible abolishment of the average contribution rate and the linking of retirement age to life expectancy.[112] In addition, at the time of the ECJ's assessment of Dutch mandatory participation, defined benefit arrangements were still the norm. With the increased shift to defined contribution arrangements, one may question whether mandatory participation in its present form still complies with the ECJ's criteria. The fact that Dutch law currently allows only Dutch funds to carry out such schemes, to the exclusion a priori of non-Dutch providers, appears difficult to maintain. The developments around the Apf, described above, might even make the justification of Dutch-style compulsory membership as a concept even more difficult to uphold. The contrast with other Member States makes the existence of this system all the more puzzling, as none of these appear have in place a formal prohibition to choose a provider from another Member State, while some even explicitly allow this.

These conclusions also apply to mandatory participation in other Member States of the EU. Having in a place a system that is ultimately liable to prohibit, impede or render less advantageous the activities of a provider of services established in another Member State[113] by implicitly or explicitly making affiliation to a provider from another Member State is forbidden. Exceptions to this prohibition are allowed only under strict conditions: they must be justified by overriding requirements relating to the public interest, be non-discriminatory and must be necessary and appropriate to attain the pursued objective. In case of direct discrimination, only the grounds enumerated in Article 52 TFEU provide reasons to justify such measures. The other Member States mentioned above do not appear to discriminate directly against providers from other Member States.

---

112   Chen and Beetsma, 'Mandatory Participation'.
113   Joined Cases C-369/96 and C-376/06.

4 The Institution for Occupational Retirement Provision (IORP) Directive[1]

4.1 Introduction

In 2003, the European legislature issued a directive on the activities and supervision of institutions for occupational retirement provision (IORPs).[2] A pension institution that qualifies as an IORP under the directive may, based on the supervision carried out in the Member State in which it is established, provide cross-border pension services (i.e. it has an IORP Passport). The IORP Directive sets a number of general solvency and financing requirements, certain investment rules (based on the prudent person principle) and general administrative and governance requirements (in particular regarding the provision of information). These general rules provide for minimum harmonization of pension entities, allowing the Member States a considerable degree of freedom to elaborate the rules on the IORP in question at national level. Consequently, this also leads to some significant differences between IORPs in different Member States. The IORP Directive of 2003 ('IORP I Directive' or 'IORPD I') has been subject to revision, and the recast directive ('IORP II Directive' or 'IORPD II') has been published in 2016 and came into force in January 2017.[3] The Member States should have implemented the IORPD II into national law and regulations by 13 January 2019.

Given the extent of the entire pension assets that are invested, IORPs, together with other financial institutions, such as, for example, banks and insurers, play an important role in financing the European economy as well as

---

1   Parts of Chapter 4.5.5-4.6 already appeared in an earlier form: P. Borsjé, H. van Meerten, 'A European Pensions Union: Towards a Strengthening of the European Pension Systems', in F. Pennings and Gijsbert Vonk (eds), *Research Handbook on European Social Security Law* (Cheltenham: Edward Elgar, 2015); P. Borsjé, H. van Meerten, 'Voorstel IORP II-richtlijn: aanzet tot hervorming van het Nederlands pensioenstelsel', *Nederlands tijdschrift voor Europees recht* 8 (2014).

2   Directive 2003/41/EC on the activities and supervision of institutions for occupational retirement provisions of 3 June 2003.

3   Directive (EU) 2016/2341 on the activities and supervision of institutions of occupational retirement provisions of 14 December 2016.

in the functioning of the European Union's capital markets. The driver behind the development of the IORP Directive in the period up to 2003 was partly to regulate the activities of the IORPs in a directive at European level, whilst at the same time strengthening the European cross-border financial market for pension institutions.[4] The IORP Directive was also intended to facilitate the cross-border provision of pensions, partly to facilitate labour mobility in the EU.

In addition, the IORP Directive was also intended to further stimulate the transition to funded retirement provision within the EU to safeguard its future sustainability in the EU Member States. Such provision is ideally suited to be organized in the framework of occupational pension arrangements. In the Netherlands and most other EU Member States, occupational pension arrangements are seen as a provision in addition (second pillar) to the basic retirement provision provided by the government (first pillar, such as the AOW, or General Old Age Pensions Act, that applies in the Netherlands).[5] From a general technical pension perspective, a funded retirement provision (administered by a pension fund, for example) seems preferable because, given the ageing population, the sustainability of systems financed on a pay-as-you-go basis will come under increasing pressure in the long term. The Dutch AOW, the first pillar provision, is generally government financed (or funded by public authorities) on a pay-as-you-go basis. In the Netherlands, the IORP Directive has largely been implemented in the Pensions Act (Pensioenwet) and the Financial Supervision Act (Wet op het Financieel Toezicht). In that regard the Dutch pension funds and premium pension institutions (PPIs) qualify as regulated IORPs within the meaning of the directive. Other European Member States have similar IORP entities.[6]

---

4   The eventual proposal for the IORP Directive therefore formed part of the Financial Services Action Plan of 1999 which, inter alia in connection with the introduction of the European currency, attempted to provide a further stimulus to the provision of financial services in the internal market. For background, see for example: http://ec.europa.eu/internal_market/finances/actionplan/index_en.htm#maincontentSec1 (link is veranderd), and J.C. van Haersolte, 'Een mammoettanker is de mistige haven van Lissabon binnengevaren: de afsluiting van het Actieplan Financiële Diensten', *Nederlands tijdschrift voor Europees recht* 5/6 en 7 (2006).

5   Apart from the first pillar and the second pillar, there are also of course individual (additional) retirement provisions (third pillar), such as, e.g., individual annuity provisions provided by insurance companies in the Netherlands and other EU Member States. Also given the wide variety of individual pension products, the analysis of this contribution focuses, as stated above, on the EU developments for the second pillar retirement provisions under the IORP Directive. In chapter 6 below the EIOPA proposal of a personal pension plan will be discussed, which can be understood as an effort to also accommodate third pillar cross-border pension solutions.

6   Luxembourg, for example, has the ASSEP and SEPCAV, Belgium the OFP. See H. van Meerten, S.N. Hooghiemstra, 'Voortschrijdend Inzicht: Pleidooi Afschaffen Pensioenbewaarder Voor Premiepensioeninstellingen', *PensioenMagazine* 6 (2018).

However, due to the differences between the national pension systems in combination with social, labour and tax legislation that differs from one country to another, there can be marked differences between these pension institutions in terms of both their socio-economic roles and their legal structures. Furthermore, in implementing the IORP Directive some Member States have consciously aimed to strengthen their own financial services sectors by facilitating the establishment of specific pension entities within their own territorial jurisdictions, which could also provide an efficient cross-border pension solution for members and (international) undertakings established in other EU Member States.[7] Taking a different approach, various Member States have also tried to shield their pension systems from European influence and, in doing so, have used the fact that the relevant social, labour and tax laws seem to be, in principle, the (almost) exclusive domain of the Member States themselves.

In developing the proposals for the IORP II Directive, the EC noted that, in a number of Member States (including the Netherlands), IORPs already play an important role in the relevant pension and social security systems. There are approximately 125,000 IORPs operating throughout the EU. The assets managed by them can be estimated at around €3 billion, even though these IORPs administer the retirement provision of just 75 million Europeans, i.e. about 20% of the entire EU employee population.[8]

4.2   Scope of the directive

The scope of the IORP II Directive (Article 2) covers IORPs with legal personality and where the IORPs does not have legal personality, those authorized entities responsible for managing them and acting on their behalf.

Clearly in line with the above-mentioned background of the IORP Directive, being developed for occupational retirement provisions and in addition to the existing European regulatory provisions already in place in the financial market, the directive also excludes entities from its scope that would already be covered by relevant EU directives and regulations, with specific reference to the applicable EU regulatory framework for the

7   Examples of this include SEPCAV (Société d'épargne-pension à capital variable) and ASSEP (Association d'épargne-pension) based in Luxembourg, OFP (Organisme voor de financiering van pensioenen) based in Belgium, and the Dutch PPIs.

8   See also European Commission, Impact Assessment on Proposal for a Directive Amending Directive 2003/41/EC on the Activities and Supervision of Institutions for Occupational Retirement Provision (2014).

investment fund market and the insurance and banking sector in full.[9] In accordance with its purpose, the directive in principle also excludes from its scope the institutions operating typical social security schemes that would fall under the EU social security regulations.[10] However an IORP would – in accordance with local social security and pension rules – also operate compulsory employment-related pension schemes that are in scope of the EU social security regulations, the IORP Directive would apply to such IORP in respect of its non-compulsory occupational retirement provision business.

Given the fundamental objective of the IORP Directive to stimulate funded pension arrangements, PAYG-based institutions are also excluded from the IORP Directive. Less obvious, however, the directive also excludes from its scope (1) institutions where employees of the sponsoring undertakings have no legal rights to benefits and where the sponsoring undertaking can redeem the assets at any time and not necessarily meet its obligations for payment of retirement benefits, and (2) companies using book-reserve schemes with a view to paying out retirement benefits to their employees. During the preparatory process of the IORP Directive it had been agreed that the IORP Directive should not have immediate material effect on existing rules and regulations for (occupational) pension arrangements and local pension market practices that were already well established. These exclusions therefore ensured that the relevant pension practices would not be affected by the IORP Directive requirements, i.e. including, for example, the widely spread book-reserve schemes that can be found in the German pension market.

Article 6 of the directive defines an IORP as:

> [A]n institution, irrespective of its legal form, operating on a funded basis, established separately from any sponsoring undertaking or trade for the purpose of providing retirement benefits in the context of an occupational activity on the basis of an agreement or a contract agreed (a) individually or collectively between the employer(s) and the employee(s) or their respective representatives, or (b) with self-employed persons, individually or collectively, in compliance with the law of the home and host Member States, and which carries out activities directly arising therefrom.

9   In this respect Article 2 of the directive refers to institutions which are covered by Directives 2009/65/EC, 2009/138/EC, 2011/61/EU, 2013/36/EU and 2014/65/EU of the European Parliament and of the Council.

10   In this respect Article 2 of the directive refers to institutions operating social security schemes which are covered by Regulations (EC) No 883/2004 and (EC) No 987/2009 of the European Parliament and of the Council.

According to the directive, retirement benefits are benefits paid by reference to reaching, or the expectation of reaching, retirement or, where they are supplementary to those benefits and provided on an ancillary basis, in the form of payments on death, disability, or cessation of employment or in the form of support payments or services in case of sickness, indigence or death. In order to facilitate financial security in retirement, these benefits usually take the form of payments for life (lifetime annuities). They may also be payments made for a temporary period or as a lump sum.

Article 4 of the IORP Directive allows Member States to choose to apply the core of the IORP Directive on cross-border pension services, solvency, investment rules, and governance and requirements on information for members and beneficiaries to the occupational retirement provision business of life insurance undertakings.[11] This effectively provides for flexibility and IORP regulation for relevant life insurance undertakings and potential access to the EU pension market. This has been opted for by, for example, France, which is also to be understood in the context of the French pension market that is structured without typical IORP entities. In accordance with Article 4 of the directive, all assets and liabilities corresponding to this business will be ring-fenced, managed and organized separately from the other activities of the insurance undertakings, without any possibility of transfer. To further accommodate local specific arrangements, Article 5 of the IORP Directive provides the option for Member States not to apply – or restrict application to some specific IORP provisions – to small IORPs. The second paragraph of Article 5 furthermore specifically indicates that provisions on investment rules (Article 19), investment management (Article 32), and requirements on asset safekeeping and depositaries (Articles 33-35) can be applied to institutions where occupational retirement provision is made under statute, pursuant to legislation, and is guaranteed by a public authority.

In accordance with the above-mentioned rules of the IORP Directive, the funded occupational pension arrangements of the EU Member States are generally brought into the IORP framework, while on the other hand, typical deviations and local pension practices are also acknowledged. Taking a closer look at the application of the above rules in respect of each Member State one also gains insight in the local differences and pension practices that can be found in the EU pension market. It is evident that the local pension markets of the Netherlands, the UK and Ireland, and (to a much lesser

11   Some Member States (e.g. France) have availed themselves of this option, while others (including the Netherlands) have not (Dutch Parliamentary Documents II, 2004/05, 30 104, No. 3).

extent) Germany, Italy and Sweden, are impacted by the IORP Directive. Member States such as Czech Republic and France that (almost) do not have local IORPs are in principle not effected, although on the basis of the IORP Directive they are required to allow IORPs from other Member States to operate and render pension services on their local pension market.[12] The provide some further insight in the local pension markets that fall outside the scope of the IORP Directive we note that pension schemes/institutions in the following Member States have excluded local arrangements from the scope of the IORP Directive with reference to Article 2, para. 2, of the directive.

Clearly, there is a broad variety of different local pension regimes and practices. Consequently, the workings and actual implications of the IORP Directive vary hugely between the relevant Member States.

4.3   General observations on the IORP Directive[13]

As stated above, pursuant to the directive, activities of an IORP must be limited to activities in connection with retirement benefits and related activities. The definition of retirement benefits in the directive for this purpose remains under the IORP II a broad one. It includes labour-related retirement benefits in the form of payments during the entire remaining life, but also temporary benefits or lump sum benefits. Furthermore, and as also indicated above, the IORP II Directive does in principle not apply to social security schemes (as defined in accordance with EU regulations) or regulated by other EU provisions (such as insurance activities under the Solvency II provisions) and institutions that operate on a PAYG basis, or where employees would (effectively) have no legal rights to benefits or to arrangements based on book-reserve schemes. Member States are free to choose the legal form of an IORP.

On the basis of the IORP I and II Directive provisions, IORPs could comprise almost all institutions that provide occupational retirement benefits, including pension funds, insurance companies (if not in scope of Solvency II Directive) and investment funds. The above-mentioned restrictions on the scope of the IORP II Directive, however, in practice result in a fragmented and unbalanced regulatory landscape for pension arrangements.

---

12   C-343/08.

13   An earlier version of parts of this paragraph – albeit about the IORP I Directive – appeared in: U. Neergaard, et al. (eds), *Social Services of General Interest in the EU* (The Hague: T.M.C. Asser Press, 2013).

First of all, the Member State option to apply the IORP II Directive to the pensions business of insurers might give rise to competitive distortions. Under the Solvency II provisions insurers are in principle subject to more strict rules and regulations – e.g. in respect of capital requirements – than IORP-regulated pension entities under the IORP II Directive. The more flexible regulatory requirements for pension funds have been an important source of tensions between the insurance and pension funds sector. The IORP II Directive furthermore does not restrict the implementation of pension schemes on a mandatory basis which in some pension market – such as in the Netherlands – might considerably restrict an open competition on pension services.

Second, the IORP II Directive exempts PAYG schemes and book reserves from its scope. This results in an unequal application to what appears to be similar schemes. For example, both in Germany and the UK pension promises have to be backed by the plan sponsor and a protection fund is in place in case a company becomes insolvent.

Third, the IORP II Directive does not allow only insurance-type vehicles within its scope, but also entities that would have the features of investment fund entities without legal personality. These kind of entities can be established as flexible arrangements – with less restrictions (e.g. in respect of governance requirements) – and straightforwardly operated by financial institutions. These arrangements would typically provide that all risks are borne by the individual investor, resembling an investment fund type of economic or beneficial ownership for investors in respect of the underlying investments. Such IORP vehicles are increasingly used for pension products that are also directly marketed to individual investors on the retail market – these kind of entities are in practice, for example, established in Malta, also in accordance with local flexible (pension and corporate law) rules and regulations.[14] An important policy question is whether it is desirable that Member States have a choice to apply the IORP Directive or the typical EU regulations for relevant investment funds (cf. the provisions under the UCITS Directive) for such individual 'pension' products.

4.3.1   Background to IORP Directive revision: On IORPs and insurers

As also discussed above, besides IORPs there are, of course, other entities as well that administer funded retirement provision in the European market.

---

14   In Malta, the retirement scheme of a contractual nature consists of a separate pool of assets with no legal personality with the purpose of providing retirement benefits. See: Legal form of the IORP, CEIOPS-DOC-08-06 Rev1, 30 October 2009.

Among these are (commercial) pension insurers which, in addition to the pension funds (and e.g. Dutch PPIs), administer employment-related (second pillar) retirement provisions in the Netherlands and other countries. Insurers have their own European supervisory regime which, over the last decade, has been thoroughly revised and laid down in the Solvency II Directive.[15] This Solvency II Directive regulates European insurance undertakings with a view to protecting insured persons (in particular individual consumers) and promoting the stability of the financial market. Inspired by the risk-based supervisory framework developed for the banking sector in the Basle Accords, the Solvency II Directive has been divided into three so-called pillars. Put briefly, this pillar structure contains the first pillar, with (quantitative) capital requirements to strengthen the solvency of insurance undertakings; the second pillar, with qualitative requirements for the (internal) control processes/governance and insurers' risk management; and the third pillar, with transparency and communication requirements for consumers and for supervisory reporting purposes.

As part of their general policy on the creation of an open EU market for financial services and activities, the EC intends to bring about a level playing field for IORPs and insurers so that all market parties can, as much as possible, participate on equal terms in a balanced European pension market. From an economic perspective, both IORPs and insurers can be regarded as providers of a financial service (i.e. a pension insurance product), entailing the obligation to safeguard the pension insurance arrangements of the individual pension members or insured persons.[16] In the proposal for the revision of the IORP Directive, to be discussed below, the EC has therefore, with the backing of advice from the EIOPA, taken inspiration from the aforementioned basic premises of the regulatory frameworks under the Solvency II Directive. In the context of the above, EIOPA had started the initiative to develop a more tailored prudential reporting and supervisory instrument for the European pension sector, reflected in their proposals for a 'holistic balance sheet', that in principle should provide transparency

---

15   Directive 2009/138/EC on the taking-up and pursuit of the business of insurance and reinsurance (Solvency II) replaces the current insurance directives (Solvency I) and entered into force as from 1 January 2016.

16   See also Recital 20 to the IORP I Directive, which has contrary to the relevant proposal from the EC has not been maintained in the IORP II Directive, cf. Recital 32, which makes specific reference to the IORPs as institutions with 'a social purpose'. Furthermore, EIOPA had advised the EC to apply the governance framework of Solvency II to IORPs as well; see EIOPA-CP-11/001, 8 July 2011.

on the funding requirements of all IORPs in the European pension market on a comparative basis.[17]

However, this approach has mainly been accompanied by criticism from the European pensions sector, which points out that, in many cases, IORPs operate as social institutions[18] without a commercial objective and are managed by the representatives of employers and employees (or employee organizations); furthermore, the governance of IORPs is often embedded in national social and labour law frameworks, and more specific 'pension law' rules. Under this approach it is assumed that the interests of pension scheme members would be 'better' served under such dedicated 'social' pension framework than if IORPs would operate on a purely commercial basis.[19]

In the light of the above debate and further lobbying by the pension sector with the support from especially the Netherlands, UK, Germany, Belgium and Ireland, the EC decided in May 2013 to take a step back and therefore not include a revised and more extensive solvency requirements in their IORP II proposal.[20] This policy move has been welcomed by the European pension market as a necessary deviation from the requirements of the Solvency II Directive framework, and thereby eliminated the most controversial subject from the agenda for an IORP Directive revision. It should be noted, however, that the EC did not drop the general principles that are also fundamental to the policy approach behind the Solvency II Directive, and so, arguably, the IORP II revision could still have (indirect) implications for the prudential regime of the IORP. This will be further discussed below.

---

17   In accordance with a market consistent approach as reflected in Solvency II Directive.

18   See, for example, the statement on IORP II by PensionsEurope (umbrella organization of European pension funds), which makes the following comment on the IORP II Proposal: 'IORPs are first and foremost social institutions', see: www.pensionseurope.eu/system/files/ PensionsEurope%20statement%20on%20IORP%20II_0.pdf. The Netherlands Pension Federation (Nederlandse Pensioenfederatie), the umbrella organization of Dutch pension funds, uses exactly the same words in its position paper on the IORP II Proposal.

19   Typically, in this respect, the Council had introduced amended wording to the recital of the IORP II Proposal, indicating that IORPs 'are pension institutions with a social purpose', which seems to exclude IORPs that would choose to (also) operate on a commercial basis. See Recital 20 of the revised IORP II Proposal; cf. also our reference above to Recital 32 of the IORP II Directive.

20   European Commission, Occupational Pension Funds (IORP): Next Steps, Memo, 23 May 2013, Brussels. On its own initiative EIOPA continued to investigate the development of a 'common framework', cf. EIOPA's Opinion to EU Institutions on a Common Framework for Risk Assessment and Transparency for IORPs, EIOPA-BoS-16/075, 14 April 2016.

4.4   Revision of the IORP Directive: IORP II

In its explanatory memorandum, the European Commission set out four specific objectives in revising the IORP Directive:[21] (1) removing remaining prudential barriers for cross-border IORPs, (2) setting requirements for good governance and risk management, (3) providing clear and relevant information to members and beneficiaries, and (4) ensuring that supervisors have the necessary tools to effectively supervise IORPs. In this regard, numbers (2) and (4) directly reflect aspects from the second pillar and the third pillar, respectively, of the aforementioned Solvency II Directive.

4.4.1   Legal basis

The legal basis of the IORP II Directive is to be found principally in the free movement of persons and services provisions and the ordinary legislative procedure (Article 114 TFEU) for the establishment of a common internal market: in principle, the measures in question in the EU are adopted by a qualified majority of the Member States.[22] Thus, the IORP Directive is and remained[23] an internal market for services directive, and competence has under the adoption of the IORP II Directive not shifted to, for example, Article 153 TFEU on social protection (in terms of, for example, working conditions), which provision may also possibly be taken into consideration in establishing pension entitlements. The fact that the IORP II Directive is not based on Article 153 TFEU is important to the European legislative process, as the measures listed under Article 153 TFEU must be adopted by the Member States unanimously, which would mean that an individual Member State could, in principle, block the adoption of this directive single-handedly.[24]

Since Article 114 TFEU remains the legal basis for the IORP II Directive, the regulation of the occupational retirement provision will thus also remain, principally, an internal market concern.[25] As set out in Chapter 2, this also has consequences for the potential scope of the directive in connection with the application of the free movement provisions under the TFEU.

---

21   See para. 1.1 of the Explanatory Memorandum to the IORP II Proposal.

22   In this regard, the IORP II Directive refers to Articles 53, 62 and 114 TFEU.

23   The legal basis of the IORP I Directive has been the same.

24   See Article 153(2) TFEU.

25   It remains to be seen whether the European Parliament also consents to using Article 114 TFEU as the basis. In the Netherlands, for example, the IORP II Proposal has been criticized; see Parliamentary Papers II 2013-2014 22 112 no 1837.

With regard to the EU legislative process of implementation of the IORP II Proposal, it seems that the EC aimed to establish the IORP II Directive with the characteristics of – what was until recently called – a Lamfalussy Directive, with the harmonized rules being adopted in four stages.[26]

In a certain sense, the Lamfalussy structure has been codified by the establishment of the three European supervisory authorities (ESAs)[27] (the European Banking Authority, European Securities and Markets Authority, and EIOPA) in combination with a modified treaty framework under the TFEU.[28] As stated in Chapter 2, the TFEU distinguishes between legislative and non-legislative acts.[29] The IORP II Proposal made reference to Article 290 TFEU, delegating to the EC the power to adopt non-legislative acts of general application to supplement or amend certain non-essential elements of a legislative act.[30] In many cases, this means that EIOPA writes the draft versions of the delegated and the implementing acts on the basis of Articles 290 and 291 TFEU.[31] After that, the European Commission (formally) ratifies these acts (also referred to as level 2.5).

As set out in Chapter 2, the preliminary stance of the Netherlands on the original IORP II Proposal as presented by the EC already contained a reservation in relation to this delegated legislation in the IORP II Directive, and moreover, under the revised IORP II Proposal, as agreed by the Council, the provisions on delegating powers for the EC have been completely deleted.[32]

26   At the first level, the Council of Ministers (made up of the national ministers) formulate the principles or frameworks, and they usually adopt them in a directive (i.e. in the context of the IORP II Proposal as well). At the second level, the Commission elaborates these principles (in technical terms as well) in directives or regulations, with the assistance of the level 2 committees (which are made up of representatives of the Member States' ministerial departments; this procedure is also referred to as 'comitology'). At the third level, the national supervisory authorities work together to advise on the rules and the implementation of supervision. These level 3 committees are made up of representatives of the supervisory authorities of all 28 EU Member States and, in this case, are therefore members of EIOPA. At the fourth level, the European legislation is implemented by the Member States, under the supervision of the European Commission, which, if necessary, can take corrective action on the basis of Article 258 TFEU.

27   M. Rötting, C. Lang, 'Das Lamfalussy-Verfahren im Umfeld der Neuordnung der europäischen Finanzaufsichtsstrukturen', *Europäische Zeitschrift für Wirtschaftsrecht* 23 (2012).

28   Agreed under the Treaty of Lisbon.

29   The relationship to the Lamfalussy structure has been summarized by H. van Meerten, A.T Ottow, 'The Proposals for the European Supervisory Authorities: The Right (Legal) Way Forward', *Tijdschrift voor financieel recht* 1.2 (2010).

30   M. Charmon, 'Comitologie onder het Verdrag van Lissabon', *Tijdschrift voor Europees en economisch recht* 2 (2013).

31   This power is generally defined in the directive itself.

32   It should be noted that besides the fear for further EU regulated solvency requirements for IORPs, the Dutch government's criticism is chiefly concerned with the increased information

This also reflects that the Netherlands had been able to successfully lobby against the introduction of (specific) EC delegating powers, under IORPD II, especially supported by other EU Member States that have more developed pension markets, seeking to protect dedicated 'social' pension frameworks, such as those in the UK, Germany and Sweden.[33]

4.4.2   Cross-border activity and applicable requirements

An internal European market, in which we all engage, works in two directions: regulating both outgoing and incoming movement. For this reason the presumption applies that similar provisions should be treated equally, regardless of the institution making the provision. This fundamental principle is the core of the EU internal market and on this basis the key to the formation of an EU pensions union.

One of the issues when providing cross-border pensions under the current Pensions Directive, is that it applies to a wide variety of institutions. That can lead to, for example, French insurers partially coming under a lighter supervisory regime than a Dutch entity executing the same pension plan as the French insurer.[34]

At the time of the revision, it had been already been widely discussed in EU pension literature that both the questions of when an institution comes under the IORP Directive as well as which regime is applicable would require further clarification.

4.4.2.1   Funding requirements and cross-border schemes
The revision should also be understood from a wider pension market perspective, where it was well appreciated that IORPD I did not have the desired results.

requirements for pension funds, which the government claims could lead to a greater administrative burden – which have been substantially limited under the revised IORP II Proposal – and the powers delegated to the EC in this regard in Article 54 of the IORP II Proposal, as deleted in the revised IORP II Proposal.

33   In November 2018, the members of the European Parliament of the Economic and Monetary Affairs Committee (ECON) have voted to agree with a proposal the EC to potentially amend the IORP II to include the instrument of 'delegated acts' in connection with requirement to integrate ESG risks (i.e. environmental, social and governance factors) in investment decisions. This proposal had been developed as part of a wider proposal to accommodate same under an amendment to the Solvency II Directive. The proposal to amend the IORP II Directive is heavily opposed by the Netherlands, Germany and Sweden and the European lobbying group for pension entities, PensionsEurope. At the time of the preparation of this chapter the outcome of this matter and relevant European legislative process was not yet know.
34   Article 4 IORP Directive.

The number of cross-border IORPs had remained modest, and the envisaged operation of market forces between European IORPs within a European pension market had not materialized. Article 16(3) of the IORPD I provides:

> In the event of cross-border activity as referred to in Article 20, the technical provisions shall at all times be fully funded in respect of the total range of pension schemes operated. If these conditions are not met, the competent authorities of the home Member State shall intervene.

Many in the European pension market perceived this (at all times) fully funded requirement as one of the greatest obstacles to IORPs developing cross-border activities between Member States. The fact is that if a pension scheme is not fully funded, sponsoring undertakings simply cannot, for example, transfer their pension scheme to an administrator in other Member States. Given the problematic state of many pension funds, this requirement can – at least potentially – have a restrictive effect.

Although an earlier, leaked draft text of the IORP II Proposal had eliminated the full funding requirement, it has nevertheless been maintained in Article 14(3) IORPD II. The 'fully funded' stipulation has, however, been clarified to some extent, where Article 14(3) also provides that in case of intervention by the competent authority of a home Member State, such competent authority shall 'require the IORP to immediately draw up appropriate measures and implement them without delay in a way that members and beneficiaries are adequately protected'. In practice, this should allow underfunded IORPs an opportunity for financial recovery also in respect of cross-border pension arrangements. Especially in cases where an IORP already operates schemes on a cross-border basis, this might give grounds for flexibility. However, in connection with the transfer of a scheme and establishment of a (new) cross-border pension arrangement, the rules could prove to be even less flexible. In such cases local supervisory authorities might find ground also with reference to more clear and restrictive requirements on cross-border pension arrangements under Article 12(7) and (8) of the IORP II Directive to use their authority to block such transfer. The IORP II Directive has bestowed the local authorities with the discretion to assess whether 'at the date of the transfer, where the transfer results in a cross-border activity', the assets to be transferred are sufficient and appropriate to cover the liabilities, technical provisions and other obligations or rights to be transferred.[35] The IORP II Directive

---

35   See also Recital 38 to the IORP II Directive.

does not provide any flexibility in case a local recovery plan is already in place – and confirmed by local supervisory authorities – for the relevant IORP that would facilitate cross-border pension services or flexibility in respect of the relevant pension scheme to be transferred to an IORP in another EU Member State. Consequently, in the case of a limited risk of underfunding of an IORP this could still pose a rather considerable barrier in the role-out of cross-border pension arrangements. This may leave substantial discretionary powers for the local authorities of the jurisdiction of the transferring host Member State (i.e. the Member State of the pension participants) and could trigger extensive (procedural) steps to establish a transfer of pension schemes. It seems that also in this respect the IORP II Directive has left room for the Member States to shield – at least to a certain extent – the existing local pension sector from cross-border pension activities.

The above has already attracted some considerable attention in some parts of the pension market. In the Dutch pension market there exists a growing interest from certain market parties to establish cross-border pension arrangements for the Dutch pension market through the use of Belgian IORP entities. This is a heavily debated subject in the Dutch pension sector and is fed by the perception within the Dutch pension sector that local Belgian supervisory and prudential requirements would not be sufficient – according to Dutch standards – to appropriately facilitate Dutch pension arrangements. From an EU perspective this debate might make a rather unbalanced impression as it has been voices from the same Dutch pension sector that in preparation of the IORP Directive revision have been heavily lobbying against the introduction of more extensive and transparent EU solvency requirements for IORPs, including whether they would be engaged in cross-border activities.

In the context of the above-mentioned debate the Dutch government had opted to implement the provisions of Article 12(3) of the IORP II Directive on the transfer of pension schemes in a rather restrictive way.[36] The text of Article 12(3) reads as follows: 'The transfer shall be subject to prior approval by [...] a majority of members and a majority of the beneficiaries concerned or, where applicable, by a majority of their representatives. The majority shall be defined in accordance with national law.'

---

36   Dutch parliamentary proceedings on the implementation of the IORP II Directive, Kamerstukken 2018-2019, nr 34934. For more detail, see H. van Meerten, L. Geerling, 'Build that wall? Het onderscheid tussen binnenlandse en grensoverschrijdende waardeoverdrachten van pensioenregelingen', *Tijdschrift recht en arbeid* 2 (2019).

As part of the Dutch implementation proposal the government introduced a specific 'two-thirds' majority requirement of all (former) pension participants of the relevant pension scheme, deliberately making a distinction between the approval regimes for cross-border transfer to a non-Dutch IORP and local Dutch transfers between local Dutch IORPs. For local transfers a rather more flexible administrative requirement would apply, based on a majority of 'two-thirds' of only the pension participant representative bodies of the relevant IORP that is facilitating the relevant pension scheme. Some Dutch market practitioners expect this restriction to result in considerable impediments for creating cross-border pension solutions in Dutch pension markets. Although this restriction is clearly in breach of the general free movement provisions under the TFEU, the Dutch government has also been advised by the Dutch Council of State that this impediment would be justified under EU law on the basis of the potential far-reaching implications for pension scheme if it would be facilitated in the context of another Member State's pension framework, without providing further basis on the specific EU case law.[37] This position has met with considerable criticism from some EU pension law experts. They argue that any such deliberate restriction on the transfer of a pension scheme to an IORP located in another Member State requires specific justification or should at least require a more proportionate approach, also in accordance with general EU law principles (i.e. only provide further measurement for local supervisory authority in case a specific concern could be sufficiently substantiated). In this respect, it should be noted that the IORP Directive specifically provides for control mechanisms for local supervisory authorities – and a communication framework with the authorities of the IORP's home Member State – in respect of the pension arrangements that are governed by their local employment and social laws and regulations. These mechanisms are aimed to effectively take away the concerns that have also been put forward by the government and recognized by the Dutch Council of State. In this respect, reference could be made to the extensive EU case law that has been produced on the extensive tax control and reporting requirements of the EU Member States that have been substantially restricted in the context of EU cross-border activities under application of the relevant European directives.[38]

---

37   See advice from the Dutch Council of State of 28 November 2018 (Dutch parliamentary proceedings, Kamerstukken I 2018-2019, 34934, nr E), also contrary to EU pension law expert opinion from Professor H. van Meerten. See also the appendix to Kamerstukken I 2018-2019, 34934, nr B.

38   See, for example, the case law in connection with Directive 76/308/EC.

4.4.2.2   Scope of cross-border regulations under IORP II

In addition to the above, in Article 6(19) of the IORPD II, the definition of 'cross-border' has been further clarified in the sense that to qualify as a 'cross-border activity' under the relevant IORP Directive provisions, it is assumed that the social and labour law that is applicable to a pension scheme must be different from the law of the territorial jurisdiction in which the IORP is established. This means, for example, that under the IORPD II, the situation in which the sponsoring undertaking and the IORP are in the same Member State does qualify as a cross-border activity if the members of the pension scheme in question are in a different Member State.

From a general EU perspective the definition of 'cross-border activity' under the IORP II Directive could be debated, especially since it excludes from its scope the situation where individual pension participants and IORPs could be resident in the same EU Member State while the employer of the pension participants – or relevant sponsoring entity to the IORP – could be located in another EU Member State. On the basis of general EU principles this clearly reflects a 'cross-border' activity, however, and would fall outside the scope of the IORP Directive regulations that apply to cross-border activities.[39] In this respect it should also be noted that in case the IORP and relevant pension participants are resident in the same EU Member State, the IORP would be under the supervision of the authorities of the same jurisdiction that would – at least in most cases – govern the employment and social law and regulatory requirements. Therefore, such shortcomings in the 'cross-border' definition under the IORP Directive should in practice expectedly not result in any complications, although it could not be ruled out that in some specific situations difficulties might arise.[40]

It should be noted that in principle the 'home Member State' (i.e. the territorial jurisdiction in which the IORP is established) plays a leading role in the supervision of the IORP established in their jurisdiction, whereby the IORP Directive aims to avoid complex exchanges of information and approval procedures between the home Member State and the 'host Member State' on the basis of straightforward communication framework, as reflected in Articles 10 and 11 of the IORPD II. In that case, the host Member State would

---

39   See in this respect the considerations of the CJEU, 16 July 2015, C-172/14.

40   For example, if the employer, located in another Member State, of the pension participants would have substantial sponsoring responsibilities, also in accordance with local social law and regulations of the home state of the IORP and the pension participants, and the relevant supervisory mechanism would require to supervisory authorities taking measures against such employer for acting in breach of these local social law and regulations.

not be allowed to impose any extra restrictions on investment policy, or prudential requirements on the IORP: such supervision would be carried out by the authorities of the home Member State of the relevant IORP pursuant to Articles 13 and 14 of the IORPD II. The host Member State would also not be allowed to impose any additional investment requirements on the home Member State either, other than already provided for under Article 19 the IORP Directive, according to Article 19(8) of the directive.

The IORP servicing cross-border pension arrangements would have to comply with the social and labour laws of the host Member State, but they would not be allowed to contain any additional prudential rules. If local social or labour laws are infringed, the national supervisory authority would have to notify the authorities of the home Member State, which would then take enforcement measures, with the local supervisory authority ultimately being able to intervene in the event of a persistent infringement of local social legislation, pursuant to Article 11(10) of the IORPD II.

Under the current IORP Directive, the 'social and labour law' that applies is almost entirely that of the Member States themselves. This, in principle, is in line with the aforementioned basis of the IORP Directive under the TFEU which, after all, is aimed at elaborating the relevant freedom of movement provisions for the establishment of an internal market – and which does not, therefore, (principally) concern the development of social protection or measures relating to employment terms.

Thus, the system of the directive is also that pension schemes are governed by the social and labour law of the Member State in which the member of the pension scheme maintains an employment relationship. In addition, under the current directive the institutions (the IORPs) are regulated by the prudential law of the Member State in which the IORP is established, with the Member State in question having to comply with certain basic norms taken from the IORP Directive.

The IORPD II also formulates a basic framework for prudential supervision, which intends to prevent legal uncertainty in this regard.

Under the IORP II Directive, Member States may no longer, or at least less easily than under the text of the IORP I Directive, create disguised national obstructions by having obvious prudential requirements included in (local) social and labour law in order to obstruct the purport of the IORP Directive in this regard. That is a major improvement. The fact is that, in the Netherlands, it was for some time possible to include the *financieel toetsingskader* (financial assessment framework), a solvency framework for pension funds, in the scope of social and labour law. That now seems to have been made impossible.

4.4.3   The prudent person principle and investment rules

As discussed above the IORP Directive as prepared in the period up to 2003 also aimed to further strengthen the advantages of cross-border investments within the EU market, based on the idea that IORPs should be treated similarly to other market investors, operating as cross-border financial service providers within a single European pension market. Consequently, the regulatory design behind the investment rules would then in principle not differ from other (commercial) financial service providers active in the insurance and investment fund market.[41] The regulations and rules within these areas had already developed on the basis of the Anglo-Saxon 'prudent person principle', which also influenced the applicable local rules on pension arrangements.[42] Moreover, at the time the IORP I Directive had been developed the prudent person principle had been a familiar principle within the most prominent EU pension markets, i.e. the UK and the Netherlands. This principle was therefore agreed upon, although under the pension regulations of some other Member States more strict investment restrictions applied for dedicated pension entities, which varied from restrictions or required allocations to particular asset classes, which could include compulsory investments in domestic markets. The IORP I Directive also provided for some basic investment rules that generally aimed to stimulate certain risk spreading investment policies and diversification.

In reflection of the financial crisis of 2008 the investment policies of pension entities have attracted further debate in the pension sector and in society in general. Furthermore, there has been an increasing focus on enhancing the availability in the financial markets of more substantial 'long-term' funding for European infrastructure projects, in particular, and, as part of the wider sustainability debate, also growing awareness of the need to take into consideration relevant environmental, social and governance (ESG) factors. These developments have been reflected in the wording of Article 19 of the IORP II Directive, which indicates that 'the assets shall be invested in the best long-term interests of members and beneficiaries as a whole'.

---

41   See, for example, Recital 6 to the IORP I Directive, and similarly Recital 46 to the IORP II Directive that reads as follows: 'By setting the prudent person rule as the underlying principle for capital investment and making it possible for IORPs to operate across borders, the redirection of savings into the sector of occupational retirement provision is encouraged, thereby contributing to economic and social progress.'

42   Article 18 of the IORP I Directive reads: 'the assets shall be invested in the best interests of members and beneficiaries'.

In public debate, some voices argue that local IORPs or financial institutions should aim to invest more prominently in domestic projects in order to stimulate, for example, local infrastructure projects. Given the general requirements for IORPs to adhere to the 'prudent person' principle any such initiatives should be weighed against 'the best long-term interests of members and beneficiaries' of the relevant pension arrangements. As also indicated above, similar restriction also apply to (commercial) insurers under the Solvency II Directive.[43]

4.4.4   System of governance and risk-management requirements

The IORP II Directive has introduced governance standards and risk-management requirements. As discussed above, these have been inspired by the forward-looking and risk-based approach also developed in the second pillar, from the Solvency II Directive for insurance undertakings.[44]

4.4.4.1   System of governance
The general governance requirements are based on the following framework, as reflected in Article 21(1) of IORPD II:

> Member States shall require all IORPs to have in place an effective system of governance which provides for sound and prudent management of their activities. That system shall include an adequate and transparent organisational structure with a clear allocation and appropriate segregation of responsibilities and an effective system for ensuring the transmission of information. The system of governance shall include consideration of environmental, social and governance factors related to investment assets in investment decisions, and shall be subject to regular internal review.

In respect of the above requirement it has also been provided that the system of governance should be proportionate to the size, nature, scale and complexity of the activities of the IORP, as per Article 21(2). In practice, however, the assessment of what would be proportionate is at the discretion

---

43 See Article 132 of the Solvency II Directive: 'Member States shall ensure that insurance and reinsurance undertakings invest all their assets in accordance with the prudent person principle.' In this respect it should be noted that under the Solvency II Directive rather extensive risk and solvency assessment provisions apply that require long-term risk factors to be addressed in their business policies, cf. Articles 45 and 209 of the Solvency II Directive.

44 See also Article 47(2) of the IORD II: 'Member States shall ensure that supervision is based on forward-looking and risk-based approach.'

of the local regulator and supervisory authorities. Especially in the more developed pension markets such the UK and the Netherlands, local rules and regulations already provide for a substantial governance framework and it remains to be seen to what extent the additional provision of the IORP II Directive will impact the governance practice of the pension sector. In any case to monitor compliance of the IORPs with the relevant governance rules the discretional powers of the local supervisory authorities are extended and the administrative burden of relevant IORPs will expectedly increase.[45]

The approach developed by the Dutch legislator and regulator under the IORP II Directive implementation proposals in the Netherlands have already had a considerable impact in the country, especially on smaller Dutch pension entities, which have had to bring their governance policies in line with the new implementation rules. This has also added to the considerable increase of compliance requirements for the Dutch pension sector over recent years. In the Dutch context this has put further pressure on the sustainability of smaller IORP entities, and from the perspective of the Dutch regulator this ties into their general policy of enhancing the further consolidation of the smaller Dutch pension entities. From a general European policy scope, the governance requirements would therefore not only bolster the proper governance systems in the pension sector as such, it might also indirectly push the agenda of the EC and EIOPA for a broader reform of the European pension sector towards more sustainable pension arrangements, especially where the initiative to create EU-regulated prudential requirements for the pension sectors still meets strong opposition from several EU Member States and the European pension sector.

In respect to the above it should be noted that the IORP II Proposal as originally presented by the EC contained the following clarification on the requirements for the persons who effective run the IORP to be 'fit' for their tasks: '[T]heir professional qualifications, knowledge and experience are adequate to enable them to ensure a sound and prudent management of the institution.' This wording required a straightforward 'professional' qualification and therefore would have meant a significant amendment to the relevant provision under the IORP I Directive, one that explicitly allows the persons without such 'professional' qualification to run IORPs and for their support to 'employ advisers with appropriate professional qualifications and experience'

---

45 As also discussed below these include, amongst others, written policies on key functions in Article 21(3), (reporting) requirements on remuneration policy in Article 23(2), the documentation of the own risk assessment in Article 28, the (notification) requirement in respect of outsourcing in Article 31(6) and the production of a pension benefit statement in Article 39, next to the general compliance and reporting obligations, as also reflected in Articles 49 through 51.

to render assistance to the IORP's management.[46] In the European pension sector, IORPs are in many cases not solely managed by persons with relevant 'professional' qualifications. For example, in the Dutch context the regulator has developed further requirements and standards to ensure more solid governance of the pension entities. The wording proposed by the EC would have resulted in a substantial shift in the profile required of persons deemed fit for IORP management positions and also create practical difficulties for the paritarian model of representation in the managerial board of (smaller) IORPs, for example, in the Dutch context. From an EC perspective, this would have placed the governance standards of the IORP more on equal footing with insurers and other (commercial) financial service providers. Upon criticism from and lobbying by the European pension sector the final wording of the IORP II Directive has been rephrased to read as follows, with reference to collective capabilities at the level of the IORP's management: 'their professional qualifications, knowledge and experience are *collectively* adequate to enable them to ensure a sound and prudent management of the IORP'.

Within the governance system of the IORP specific control and reporting should be implemented to enable the management and the supervisory body of the IORP to ensure a proper operational and risk decision-making process. To achieve the above, written policies should be developed by the IORP that relate to risk management, internal audit and – where relevant – actuarial and outsourced activities, also mirrored in the so-called 'key functions' for risk management, internal audit and actuarial functions that the IORP should then have in place.[47]

Furthermore, Article 23 of the IORP II Directive also includes provisions on remuneration policy, indicating – amongst others – that the remuneration policy shall be in line with the long-term interests of members and beneficiaries of pension schemes operated by the IORP. Information on these policies should in principle also be regularly publicly disclosed.

4.4.4.2   Risk-management requirements

In respect of risk management, Article 25(1) of the IORP II Directive requires the following:

> Member States shall require IORPs, in a manner that is proportionate to their size and internal organization, as well as to the size, nature, scale and complexity of their activities, to have in place an effective risk-management

---

46   See Article 9(1)(b) of the IORP I Directive.
47   See Articles 21 and 24 of the IORP II Directive.

function. That function shall be structured in such a way as to facilitate the functioning of a risk-management system for which the IORPs shall adopt strategies, processes and reporting procedures necessary to identify, measure, monitor, manage and report to the administrative, management or supervisory body of the IORP regularly the risks, at an individual and at an aggregated level, to which the IORPs and the pension schemes operated by them are or could be exposed, and their interdependencies. That risk-management system shall be effective and well-integrated into the organizational structure and in the decision-making processes of the IORP.

The IORP II Directive also indicates a set of specific areas that should be covered by the risk management system of an IORP, which include underwriting and reserving, asset-liability management and investment (specific attention to derivatives and securitization and similar commitments), next to liquidity and concentration risk, and operational risk management, and insurance and other risk mitigation techniques, and ESG risks relating to the investment profile, and management thereof.

Not surprisingly the above-mentioned risk-management system under the IORP II Directive seem to resemble the risk-management approach that has also been developed under the Solvency II Directive. Furthermore, the IORP Directive also introduces under Article 28 an 'own risk assessment', which seems to resemble the 'own risk and solvency assessment' (ORSA) under the Solvency II Directive. In this respect the 'own risk assessment' should – amongst others – include an assessment of the effectiveness of the risk-management system, further enhancing an appropriate strategy behind the relevant risk-management policies and the decision-making process of the IORP. The own risk assessment should be performed by the IORP at least every three years, 'proportionate to the size and internal organization as well as to the size, nature, scale and complexity of their activities'. As also mentioned above, the reference to a proportionate approach would in practice still leave a considerable amount of discretionary power to the regulator, also in view of the specific appreciation of relevant local prudential standards as well as employment and social law requirements.

Moreover, the own risk assessment should also include 'an assessment of the overall funding needs of the IORP, including a description of the recovery plan where applicable', and 'an assessment of the risks to members and beneficiaries relating to the paying out of their retirement benefits', also with reference to 'indexation mechanism' and 'benefit reduction mechanisms'.[48]

---

48   See Article 28(2)(d) and (e) of the IORPD II.

And although the IORP II Directive does not introduce more specific solvency requirements as such – see also the paragraphs below – the above directly implies that a substantial analysis on the solvency position of the IORP should be produced by the IORP, in accordance with IORPD II requirements. Since no specific clarification has been provided under the IORPD II, it might be that EIOPA and the EC publish further recommendations in this respect, which in turn could also give ground reinitiate discussions on the introduction of a 'holistic balance sheet' or similar comparative reporting format.[49] Also given the general policy objectives from the EC indicated above, the requirements on risk management and own risk assessment might create a framework with potentially further consequences for the IORP's operations and financial requirements.

Article 31 of the IORP II Directive provides for further requirements on outsourcing of certain activities, including key functions and management of the IORP. Pursuant to Article 31(3) outsourcing should not be undertaken if it would result in (1) impairing the quality of the system of governance of the IORP, (2) unduly increasing the operational risk, (3) impairing the ability of the competent authorities to monitor the compliance of the IORP, or (4) undermining continuous and satisfactory service to members and beneficiaries. This provision includes requirements of notification to the competent authority 'in a timely manner' on any outsourcing of activities, and powers for the competent authorities to request information thereon. In practice, this may result in considerable additional administrative requirements for IORPs, creating further means for a regulator to intervene and control the outsourcing plans of an IORP. In the Dutch context the regulator has indicated to more closely monitor the outsourcing of activities, also requiring additional safeguards and sufficient countervailing power at the level of the IORP in relation to its external service provider. In line with our observations above, the outsourcing requirements under the IORP II Directive might have considerable consequences, especially for smaller Dutch IORPs.

4.4.5 Information requirements and supervisory instruments

Before further addressing the information requirement provisions and the supervisory instruments under the IORPD II, we will first provide

---

49 It should be noted that the wording of Article 28 seems to imply that the own risk assessment includes a full quantitative analysis, with the exception of a 'qualitative assessment of the mechanism protecting retirement benefits, including, as applicable, guarantees', indicated under Article 28(2)(f) of the IORPD II.

some further background on the specific considerations that should be understood to understand the EC's initial approach on the relevant matter and its proposal for the revised IORP Directive.

4.4.5.1   Pensions and fundamental European rights

Although the IORP Directive is based on the strengthening of the EU common market with specific regard to the free movement of persons and services provisions, the EC has not only substantiated the revision of the IORP Directive in strictly economic terms. The EC indicated that their proposal to revise the IORP II Directive is in line with Europe 2020, a strategy formulated by the European Council with the objective of establishing a sustainable, competitive as well as social market economy through structural reforms.[50]

In its explanatory memorandum to the IORP II Proposal, the EC puts forward a highly fundamental consideration. Referring to the Charter of Fundamental Rights of the European Union (the 'Charter', see below), the EC states that the IORP II Proposal promotes human rights by protecting retirement benefits. The EC furthermore indicates that the proposal will have a positive impact on consumer protection and freedom to conduct business, 'in particular by ensuring a higher level of transparency of retirement provisioning, informed personal financial and retirement planning as well as facilitating cross-border business of IORPs and their sponsors'.[51] In the explanatory memorandum the EC also expressly draws attention to the problem that many European IORP members are not aware that their pension entitlements could be cut. In this respect the EC makes explicit reference to the situation in the Netherlands, also indicating that IORP members would not have a proper understanding of the costs incurred for managing their pension schemes.[52] With reference to fundamental European rights, the EC proves to be a critical observer of more traditional pension systems that are strongly founded on the principle of solidarity, which is also relevant for the pension system in the Netherlands. Pursuant to the Dutch Pensions Act, an industry-wide pension fund operates as a collective on the basis of solidarity, in fact fully sharing insurance costs without the *ex*

---

50   See also the findings in C-341/05.

51   See para. 1.2 of the Explanatory Memorandum to the IORP II Proposal, with reference to Articles 25, 38 and 16, respectively, of the Charter of Fundamental Rights of the European Union. The EC also notes that the general objective also, in fact, justifies 'certain limitations on the freedom to conduct a business (Article 16)'.

52   See para. 11 of the Explanatory Memorandum to the IORP II Proposal.

ante establishment of purely transparent individual rights.[53] The recovery and curtailing system of the traditional Dutch pension funds which, in the perception of many members, exhibits little transparency and unequally shifts the burden to a younger generation, plays, for example, a major role in the debate about the reform of the current Dutch pension system.[54] Thus, the aforementioned fundamental EU rights underpinning the IORP II Proposal should also be part of the current discussion about the reform and the sustainability (under European law) of the local pension systems of the Member States, including the Dutch pension system.[55]

4.4.5.2 Guarantees

In practical terms, 'cutting' pension entitlements only applies to rights that, in principle, have been assigned unconditionally ('guaranteed') – a guarantee that is similar to the way in which pension insurance members can expect a guaranteed pension benefit. Within the pensions sector, such schemes are called defined benefit (DB) schemes. The capital reserves required for such pension funds and other IORPs (as well as for commercial insurers) should, if the returns on the investments are insufficient, ensure that the pension entity can fulfil the obligations it has guaranteed to the member for as long as possible. It should be noted that, under the requirements of the Solvency II Directive, insurers are obliged to guarantee their obligations with a higher degree of certainty than IORPs under the current IORP Directive. This means that DB arrangements serviced by commercial insurers' are currently more expensive (or potentially so), but also backed up by greater financial safeguards.[56]

Schemes that are not guaranteed or 'insured' and whose entitlements are, in principle, directly influenced by the underlying investment

---

53   This is also expressed in the prohibition against legal 'ring-fencing' by Dutch industry-wide and company pension funds, see section 123 of the Dutch Pensions Act. An exception to this is provided for PPIs, which may ring-fence schemes; however, this is subject to the restriction that PPIs may not bear biometric risks and, in the Dutch context, are effectively only allowed to administer defined contribution schemes (see also below).

54   See also Article 48 of the IORP II Proposal, subsequently reflected in Article 39 of the revised IORP II Proposal, which addresses this issue.

55   We note that this could also have consequences for the legal assessment of the conversion – often referred to as *'invaren'* (conversion) in the Dutch pension debate – of existing pension entitlements into a new structure containing modified pension entitlements which, under the right to property set out in Article 17 of the EU Charter, could in principle be questionable.

56   Put simply, insurers are obliged to maintain a 99.5% value at risk (VaR) (i.e. theoretical insolvency occurring once every 200 years), whilst the Dutch pensions sector, for example, maintains a 97.5% VaR (i.e. theoretical insolvency occurring once every 40 years). Bridging this difference could entail considerable extra costs (of contributions) for members, especially in light of the already low funding ratios of many pension funds.

results are called defined contribution (DC) schemes. In such schemes, the members directly bear all risks (i.e. both the positive and negative results) of the investments related to their pension entitlements and, in principle, no funding shortfall can occur. Previously, the majority of arrangements offered in the Netherlands were DB schemes; given the higher costs entailed in maintaining greater capital reserves, many parties feel a growing need for DC schemes. This trend can also be clearly seen in the rest of Europe.[57] However, many Dutch pension funds (and insurers) still maintain the DB schemes begun in the past, and in many sectors DB schemes are still seen as the norm for a 'certain' kind of pension. The big Dutch industry-wide pension funds are still mainly geared towards providing DB schemes.

During the financial and economic crisis starting in 2008, capital reserves proved to be insufficient and many Dutch pension funds were no longer able to fulfil their obligations: the 'certainty' of the guaranteed DB schemes turned out to be merely relative. In the Dutch literature, the actual performance of the pension funds' applied curtailing and recovery system compared with the safeguards provided in the Dutch Pensions Act and the provisions of the current IORP Directive had already been analyzed.[58] If a scheme is underfunded, the IORP Directive includes a recovery system for IORPs, but the actual wording of the directive does contain restrictions. The recovery system set out in the IORP I Directive seems to seek to recover the amount of appropriate assets in order to fully cover the technical provision, whilst the 'cutting' of entitlements in the Dutch context results in a reduction of the pension liabilities on the pension fund's balance sheet.[59] Putting it cautiously, it does not seem to be unreservedly clear whether the current Dutch curtailing and recovery system for DB schemes can

57   It should be noted here that, in recent years, investment strategies have been developed that have de facto limited the potential 'risks' for members of DC schemes, as the opportunities for benefiting from higher investment returns are potentially higher in DC schemes and thus certain risks, including market risks (for example, inflation), which cannot unreservedly be avoided in DB commitments, can in fact be offset.

58   Under the Dutch Pensions Act, curtailing of benefits is, in principle, an *ultimum remedium* (see section 134 of the Dutch Pensions Act), although this is subject to certain caveats; see, for example, P.J.M. Akkermans, 'Korten, afstempelen, versoberen, verminderen: de 'kleine lettertjes' onder de loep', *PensioenMagazine* 22 (2011); J.A. Gielink, L.J.P. van der Meij, M.W. Minnaard, E.M.F. Schols, and M.C.J. Witteman, 'Juridische aspecten van korten van pensioenen', *Tijdschrift voor Pensioenvraagstukken* 8 (2011).

59   See Article 16 of the IORP Directive; here the directive seems to assume a 'short-term' recovery to 100% cover, whilst the recovery system of Dutch pension and supervisory legislation assumes 'minimum' cover of (approx.) 105%, to be attained within a number of years.

be entirely applied in accordance with the IORP I Directive. In the Dutch literature, the power to curtail has been defended with a reference to (inter alia) Article 9(3) of the IORP Directive, which provides: 'A Member State may make the conditions of operation of an institution located in its territory subject to other requirements, with a view to ensuring that the interests of members and beneficiaries are adequately protected.'[60] However, in the IORP II Proposal this very provision had been deleted from the text of the directive. This is in line with the EC's approach to adding transparent, stricter conditions in the revised directive to rules that can directly affect the position of the individual member of a pension scheme.

This issue is also addressed in Article 37 of the IORPD II, which provides that Member States should ensure that the members and beneficiaries of domestic IORPs are sufficiently informed about the following elements, amongst others: (1) the nature of the financial risks borne by the members and beneficiaries, (2) the conditions regarding full or partial guarantees under the scheme or of given level of benefits, and (3) the mechanisms protecting accrued entitlements or the benefit reduction mechanism, if any. This provision clearly focuses on the protection entitlements of the individual member, also reflecting the main objective of prudential supervision under Article 45(1) of the IORPD II.[61] This raises the question to what extent, for example, the current rather complex Dutch curtailing and recovery system, on a collective basis embedded in 'solidarity', will remain sustainable under European law, i.e. under the revised IORP Directive.

4.4.5.3   Funding requirements

The approach to 'guarantees' is obviously directly linked to the most important issue that the EC has for the time being refrained from tackling in the IORP II Proposal: formulating stricter ('quantitative') funding requirements for strengthening the solvency of IORPs. The fact is that the required level of capital reserves directly affects the way in which an IORP is able to fulfil and continue fulfilling its obligations and thus the extent to which the cutting of 'guaranteed' pension entitlements can be avoided. This also applies to the funding of Dutch pension funds.

As stated above, in preparing the IORP II Proposal the EC intended, among other things, to use the regulatory insurance framework of the Solvency

---

60   See J.A. Gielink, L.J.P. van der Meij, M.W. Minnaard, E.M.F. Schols, and M.C.J. Witteman, 'Juridische aspecten van korten van pensioenen', *Tijdschrift voor Pensioenvraagstukken* 8 (2011).
61   Under the original IORP II Proposal as presented by the EC, draft Article 48(2) more explicitly required that the IORP would inform the members on the 'nature of the guarantee'.

II Directive as its guideline. This elicited criticism from, in particular, the Dutch and English, as well as, for example, the Irish and German pension sectors. Fearing higher funding requirements, they were also concerned about overly tight regulation under a revised IORP Directive. These countries have for considerable time already had a (more or less) reasonably developed funded system, with many DB schemes. The criticism was generally that, copying the high level of certainty for DB schemes which is required under the Solvency II Directive for insurers (including pension insurers) was not feasible for IORPs in the pensions sector without considerable cost increases (in the absence of a statutory possibility of reducing the DB entitlements, the higher capital reserves would have to be generated from, inter alia, higher pension contributions). It was also pointed out that the legal structuring of guarantees in the pensions sector is strongly dependent on the national (often specifically referred to as social and labour) law applicable to an IORP. In some cases, for instance, the solvency of pension funds can be bolstered by sponsor commitments (e.g. a statutory obligation on the employer to pay in additional funds), thus offsetting possible underfunding of the pension liabilities; and, as discussed above, in the Netherlands it is, in principle, possible on certain conditions to cut pension entitlements in order to bring the pension fund's financial position back into balance.[62] Following this, in 2012-2013 at the Commission's request EIOPA also began a further investigation into the development of funding requirements with the application of a 'holistic balance sheet' or 'common framework', in which the flexibility used to determine the solvency of an IORP was, where possible, incorporated into a model. This so-called Quantitative Impact Study (QIS) appeared on the one hand to further confirm the desire of the EC (and EIOPA) to develop funding requirements but, on the other hand, it also concluded that, given the complexity of the applied model and the fact that the investigation had been a preliminary one, it would be wise to spend more time studying the matter in further detail before presenting new rules in this regard.[63]

The measures proposed by the EC and EIOPA on the basis of the draft IORP II Directive did not appear to include any new funding requirements,

---

62   In this regard the Dutch Ministry of Social Affairs and Employment actually put it to EIOPA that the Dutch 'guaranteed' (DB) schemes should be viewed internationally as DC schemes.
63   In certain cases, with the application of the model potentially considerable shortfalls in IORPs were discovered; see EIOPA, 'QIS on IORPs: Preliminary Results for the EC', EIOPA-BoS-13/021, 9 April 2013, and 'Report on QIS on IORPs', EIOPA-BoS-13/124, 4 July 2013; the Commission's response followed on 23 May 2013; see the EC, 'Occupational Pension Funds (IORP): Next Steps', MEMO/13/454, 23 May 2013. In May 2016 EIOPA published its opinion paper on this matter.

but new developments in this regard could in respect of the IORP Directive not entirely be ruled out, which we will further discuss below.[64]

As also mentioned above, under the final wording of the IORP II Directive, as agreed by the Council, the provisions on delegating powers for the EC have been deleted, including the deletion of draft Article 30 on delegated acts for the risk evaluation for pensions, in connection with concerns of some Member States (e.g. the Netherlands and the UK) on additional funding requirements as discussed above.

The above is arguably not in line with the general financial and economic policies as adopted over the recent years within the EU. On the basis of European case law, it can be noted that the solvency difficulties of the pension funds could also have consequences for the position and liability of the Member States and their public supervisory authorities and, possibly, financial consequences as well.[65] This could therefore also be a reason to further reinforce the role of the EC and EIOPA in this regard.

4.4.5.4 Information requirements and supervision under the IORP II Directive

As also discussed above, to enhance communication and the sharing of accurate information, the IORP II Directive introduces new requirements on information to provided to the members and beneficiaries of the IORP, as reflected in Articles 36 through 44 of IORPD II.[66]

This includes a standard format for the annual communication on a set specific to the relevant pension arrangement, the so-called 'pension benefit statement', pursuant to Article 38.[67] The pension benefit statement provides information on the pension benefit projections and entitlements and on the

---

64 In principle this could effected on the basis of delegated powers for the EC in this respect, however, the draft text of Article 30 ('Delegated act for the risk evaluation for pensions') of the IORP II Proposal from the EC already empowered the EC to adopt delegated acts. See para. 3.4 of the Explanatory Memorandum to the IORP II Proposal, 'Detailed Explanation of the Proposal', Regarding Article 30 in Chapter 1 (System of Governance). As also mentioned above, in November 2018 a proposal to amend the IORPD II to create delegated acts for ESG risk-management purposes has been agreed by ECON.

65 C-398/11. In the *Hogan* case the CJEU ruled in essence that, if employers become insolvent, there has to be a minimum guarantee for members of occupational pension schemes. If a pension fund pays out less than 49% of the amount of the pension benefit that was originally promised, then the Member State may be liable for the shortfall on the basis of (inter alia) the Insolvency Directive (2008/94/EC).

66 In this respect, reference has already been made to Article 37 of the IORD II.

67 This 'pension benefit statement' is somewhat similar to the Dutch *uniform pensioenoverzicht* (uniform pension statement).

amount of paid pension contributions and breakdown of costs deducted by the IORP.[68] Further general information requirements are also introduced in Articles 41 through 44, especially for the benefit of prospective members of a relevant pension scheme and of beneficiaries during the pay-out phase.

Resembling the requirements under the third pillar of the Solvency II Directive, IORPD II contains prudential supervisory rules laid down in Articles 45 through 51 of IORPD II. As discussed above, the EC had consciously refrained from introducing any straightforward solvency requirements in their IORP II Proposal. The wording of Articles 45, 46 and 47, however, seem to reflect rather closely the forward-looking and risk-based principles that are at the core of the solvency requirements under the Solvency II Directive.

Article 45(1) identifies the protection of the rights of the members and beneficiaries as the main objective of prudential supervision. In the light of the above considerations this can be understood as a key notion of the prudential supervision under IOPRD II. In fact, it substantiates that any action from the competent authorities would in principle be weighed against the purpose of protecting a members or beneficiary of the IORP, and consequently would justify a rather severe prudential supervisory actions and compliance burden at the level of the IORP. Although the European pension sector might be understood as having the protection of the members and beneficiaries as the main focus of its policies, its lobbying activities are in addition also explicitly aimed to protect the operations of the continuity of the pension sector as such, which, for example, is reflected in a statement in a position paper of the EIOPA Occupational Pensions Stakeholder Group: 'EIOPA is rightly speaking of "protection of members and beneficiaries". We note that in the field of occupational pensions "member/stakeholder protection" ought to be the right wording.'[69]

Furthermore Article 46 requires that the Member States shall ensure prudential supervision on – amongst others – the (funding of) technical

---

68 See Articles 36 through 44 of the IORPD II.

69 See Position Paper of the EIOPA Occupational Pensions Stakeholder Group on EIOPA's Opinion to EU Institution on a Common Framework for Risk Assessment and Transparency for IORPs, EIOPA-OPSG-17-2, 13 January 2017, consideration 90, which in full reads as follows: 'EIOPA is rightly speaking of "protection of members and beneficiaries". We note that in the field of occupational pensions "member/stakeholder protection" ought to be the right wording, whereas we have the impression that this is sometimes mixed up with "consumer protection". It is important that such protection does not burden the IORP or sponsor such that benefits are reduced and members/beneficiaries end up with less.' This final observation of the OPSG seems to identify a certain independent interest of the IORP superseding the individual interest of the members and beneficiaries, presumably with reference to the concept of 'solidarity'.

provisions, regulatory own funds, and the available and required solvency margins, but also on the system of governance and information to be provided to members and beneficiaries, which also again reflects the principles of the Solvency II Directive.[70] With reference to the observations made above on the background of the EC's proposal for the revision of the IORP Directive, it can be understood that Article 47(5) reads as follows: 'Member States shall ensures that the competent authorities duly consider the potential impact of their actions on the stability of the financial systems in the Union, in particular in emergency situations.' This might give ground to substantiate and undertake rather extraordinary measures to establish the objectives of the IORP Directive, i.e. protecting the rights of the members and beneficiaries.

Articles 48 through 51 relate to the compliance and reporting obligations of an IORP vis-à-vis the competent authorities, including their powers of intervention, and an overview of the specific elements of the supervisory review process. It also clarifies that the supervisory review under IORPD II does not consist only of an assessment of the system of governance and risk (management) at the level of the IORP. Article 49(1)(c) and 49(3) also specify that competent authorities shall have 'monitoring tools, including stress-tests, that enable them to identify deteriorating financial conditions in an IORP and to monitor how a deterioration is remedied' and, pursuant to 49(3), 'shall have the necessary powers to require IORPs to remedy weakness or deficiencies identified in the supervisory review process'. This effectively requires the competent authorities to be proactively involved in monitoring IORPs in order to prevent financial difficulties at the level of an IORP, and act with full discretionary powers to enforce a proper recovery process of an IORP.

The above-mentioned comprehensive set of information requirements and supervisory instruments could be expected to result in an additional administrative burden for the European pension sector.[71] Moreover, the IORPD II rules on prudential supervision clearly establish a rather considerable responsibility for the Member States and their competent authorities to ensure the proper management and financial soundness of its pension

---

70   See Articles 45(1) and 46 of the IORPD II.

71   In context of the Netherlands, however, a similar information sharing mechanism has already been implemented and therefore the IORP II Directive should not have significantly change current Dutch pension practice in this respect. On the basis of the wording of the initial IORP II Proposal of the EC, it had been fears the relevant provisions could bring additional costly paperwork without focus on effective communications with the relevant scheme members and beneficiaries.

sector. Furthermore, in the light of the EU case law (cf. *Hogan*) this could have financial consequences for the Member States as well.[72] In the context of the above it might be that some local policymakers in relevant Member States would seek to introduce additional solvency requirements for their domestic IORPs, in order to create stability and sustainability of the pension arrangements, in line with the policy aims of the EC, thereby in fact indirectly establishing an EU regulated solvency regime for the pension sector.

4.5   Freedom of movement safeguarded?

The recitals to the IORPD II state that everyone must be free to transfer a pension scheme to a different Member State, in the context of the provisions of the IORPD II, subject to authorization from the authorities of the Member State in which the IORP is established and – especially in respect of the social and labour law items – the authorities of the Member State of the transferring IORP.[73] Thus, if a Dutch pension scheme is transferred to a Belgian IORP, the Belgian supervisory authority may oppose this, and, under certain conditions, the Dutch supervisory authority could withhold authorization. Furthermore, as discussed above, permission from the pension fund stakeholders should also be obtained, to the extent required by Dutch law. However, due to Dutch national social and labour law, which under the IORP II Directive remains at the discretion of the Member States, it will still not be possible to withdraw from a compulsory industry-wide pension fund.[74]

The question is to what extent the Dutch system of compulsory membership results in an unauthorized obstacle to the free movement of persons and services. According to the literature, with references to the relevant EU case law, compulsory membership may be justified on the basis of the 'rule of reason' and the social function of a pension fund in accordance with the principle of solidarity.[75] On this basis, however, the ECJ has held that the relevant compulsory (social) insurance arrangements that are administered by institutions which, in principle, are subject to public supervision and which do not – at least not by definition – operate

---

72   C-398/11.
73   See Recitals 11 and 12 of the IORPD II.
74   See also Recital 35 and Article 11(1) of the IORPD II and Article 20(1) of the IORPD I.
75   C-350/07.

as independent undertakings, are justified. In principle, however, Dutch industry-wide pension funds operate as independent undertakings and administer compulsory retirement provision also in the context of collective bargaining arrangements which have been agreed by the social partners. According to the *Laval* judgement, an obstacle to the freedom of movement which is the result of collective bargaining arrangements would be less readily justified than measures initiated by the Member State itself (or through its intervention).[76] Therefore, insofar as the compulsory pension arrangements are implemented in the context of collective bargaining arrangements, it might be doubtful whether compulsory membership as an obstacle to the freedom of movement provisions can be justified under the TFEU.[77] Also with reference to the considerations put forward by the EC to their IORP II Proposal on the transparency of the pension system in accordance with the EU Charter, the question can therefore be raised whether, given the current social and economic developments, compulsory membership in combination with the solidarity principle in the form of the Dutch average contribution system is still the most appropriate way of organizing additional pensions in the second pillar.

4.6   Tax aspects

In general, the different tax treatment of pension schemes in the Member States concerned is also seen as a considerable obstacle to establishing a common pension market in the EU. In practice it can, for example, be difficult for a pension scheme, designed according to the law of one Member State, to comply with the requirements for applying a tax facility in another Member State. And in some cases the operation of various tax regimes of various Member States can, for example, result in double taxation because both the country where the member of the pension scheme (formerly) worked and the country where that recipient of retirement benefits (currently) lives, taxes the income (as the pension is accrued in a different Member State from the one in which (following emigration) retirement benefits are received). In practice, double taxation in such cases can only be prevented (or mitigated) if the Member States in question have concluded a treaty to prevent double

---

76   C-438/05, *Viking.*

77   In this regard, an industry-wide pension fund must, under the Dutch Pensions Act, always be structured as a Dutch entity. This constitutes as such an illegitimate exclusion of service providers from other Member States.

taxation. Apart from the treatment of pension schemes, the tax treatment of the pension entities themselves (which may qualify as IORPs) also plays a role. Pension entities are often accorded tax-favourable treatment – for instance, an exemption from income and capital gains taxation. Facilities that can limit taxation are also often applicable to the entities in which the pension institutions invest (e.g. investment funds). Given the fact that investments are often made across borders and investment structures are thus subject to various tax regimes, international investment structures in particular (also within the EU) are far from always being entirely tax neutral.[78]

The tax aspects are left intact under the recent revision of the IORP Directive. The fact is that under the TFEU taxation, in principle, seems the exclusive domain of the Member States, while harmonizing measures are only permissible if they are adopted unanimously.[79] On the other hand, under the TFEU the national tax policy and legislation of the Member States must be in accordance with the provisions on free movement, thus safeguarding the basic premise that cross-border activities and purely national activities be accorded equal treatment (including equal tax treatment). This means, for example, that the payment of pension contributions to an IORP established in another Member State must come under the same tax facility as the payment of pension contributions to a local IORP. On the other hand, double taxation (of, for example, retirement benefits received) cannot therefore, in principle, be avoided in all cases.[80] In the past, the EC has taken initiatives to achieve further harmonization on the taxing of pensions, but it has not yet adopted any more far-reaching measures.[81]

---

78   Cf. the observations regarding the UCITS in EIOPA's Towards an EU-single market for personal pensions. An Preliminary Report to COM, EIOPA-BoS-14/029, February 2014, pp. 34-35. In this regard see also, for example, P. Borsjé, W. Specken, 'Taxation and Cross-Border Pooling in the EU Pension Sector: From UCITS to IORP', *Derivatives & Financial Instruments* 15.5a (2013).

79   See, for example, Article 114, para. 2 TFEU.

80   (Additional) taxation that is imposed when the value of pension entitlements is, upon emigration, transferred to another Member State can also pose an obstruction to worker mobility within the internal market. Nor does the current proposal for the Portability Directive (Amended Proposal for a Directive of the European Parliament and of the Council on Minimum Requirements for Enhancing Worker Mobility by Improving the Acquisition and Preservation of Supplementary Pension Rights, COM/2007/0603 final – COD 2005/0214), provide (full) protection.

81   See, for example, the communication from the EC entitled 'The Elimination of Tax Obstacles to the Cross-border Provision of Occupational Pensions', COM (2001) 214, 19 April 2001.

4.7   Final observations

Even after its recent revision the regulatory framework of the IORP Directive clearly has it shortcomings. Further steps, however, have been undertaken to enhance the servicing of cross-border pension arrangements, and to provide further regulatory requirements in respect of governance and transparency, which are also embedded in additional prudential supervisory rules and generally reflect the approach developed under the Solvency II Directive. In this respect it seems that the IORP II Directive is a prominent building bloc on the way of creating an EU pensions union.

5 Application of EU law on pensions: The property issue[1]

5.1 Introduction

Since entry into force of the Charter of Fundamental Rights of the European Union in 2009,[2] it can be argued that all of the European Union's general principles of law are essentially 'covered.' The Charter codifies, directly or indirectly, all existing EU fundamental rights and legal principles.[3] According to Barents and Brinkhorst, it can even be stated that the Charter must always be applied by the ECJ as well as the national courts.[4] This seems to follow the reasoning set out in Faber,[5] in which the ECJ held that when an EU legal norm is used as a rule of public order in an internal legal system and is of the same order as a national rule, the national courts are required to test each provision which is transposed into national law against the EU norm.

In this chapter we want to address the property rights issue, a fundamental right both covered by the Charter and the ECHR.

5.2 Article 17 Charter and Article 1 FP ECHR

While both the Charter and the ECHR offer protection of personal ownership rights, the application may differ.

In this particular case, it is important to compare Article 1 EP of the ECHR and Article 17 of the Charter. Article 17(1) of the Charter reads:

Everyone has the right to own, use, dispose of and bequeath his or her lawfully acquired possessions. No one may be deprived of his or her possessions, except in the public interest and in the cases and under the conditions provided for by law, subject to fair compensation being paid

---

1   Part of this chapter appeared in the EJSS as P. Borsjé, H. van Meerten, 'Pension Rights and Entitlement Conversion ('*Invaren*'): Lessons from a Dutch Perspective with Regard to the Implications of the EU Charter', *European Journal of Social Security* 18 (2016).
2   Charter of Fundamental Rights of the European Union (2012) OJ C326.
3   It can be argued that the Charter can be read to 'include' all 'national' principles of law.
4   Barents and Brinkhorst, *Grondlijnen*.
5   C-479/13 (Faber).

in good time for their loss. The use of property may be regulated by law in so far as is necessary for the general interest.

However, it should be noted that in Dutch policy papers[6] and literature it has been argued (see also further below)[7] that the conversion of pension rights does not need to be tested against the Charter in addition to testing it against Article 1 FP ECHR, as such a test would presumably lead to the same results. After all, Article 17 Charter and Article 1 FP ECHR in principle correspond, as is confirmed by the explanatory memorandum to the Charter.

Before we turn to the differences between the two articles, it should be noted that both Article 17 Charter and Article 1 FP ECHR seem to constitute a 'right' and not a 'principle'. In the case of *Skorkiewicz v Poland*, the ECtHR[8] held that:

> The Court recalls that the making of contributions to a pension fund may, in certain circumstances, create a property right and such a right may be affected by the manner in which the fund is distributed. [...] The Court further recalls that the rights stemming from paying contributions to social insurance systems are pecuniary rights for the purposes of Article 1 of Protocol No. 1 to the Convention.

Seen against this background, it seems likely that the payment of contributions to a pension fund creates a property right in the sense of Article 1 FP ECHR and, *eo ipso*, Article 17 Charter. That alone, together with the clear and precise reading of Article 17 Charter, makes it sufficiently clear and precise, unconditional and capable of producing rights for individuals. In other words, Article 17 Charter seems, under the circumstances, capable of

---

6   The report 'Collective Pension Right and Entitlement Conversion' of the Dutch Ministry of Social Affairs and Employment notes the following: 'The contents and scope of Article 17 of the Charter are the same as those of Article 1 FP ECHR. This is evident, too, from the explanatory memorandum issued along with the Charter. This means that the same elements are important for a test against this provision, meaning that hereafter a test against Article 1 FP ECHR suffices.' The Dutch Council of State is of the opinion that 'Article 17 of the Charter has the same meaning and scope as the Article 1 of the Protocol to the ECHR' (Dutch Council of State, Uitspraak 201203862/1/A3, 14 August 2013, http://www.raadvanstate.nl/uitspraken/zoeken-in-uitspraken/ tekst-uitspraak.html?id=75343, p. 4.2 (our translation).

7   For example: R.H. Maatman, 'Invaren, invaarproblematiek en tussenvariant', *Tijdschrift voor Pensioenvraagstukken* 2 (2014).

8   ECtHR, *Skorkiewicz v Poland* (1999), Application No. 34610/97.

having a direct horizontal effect. This means that the Charter may provide protection against breaches of a fundamental right by an IORP.

5.2.1 Different wording

From a general perspective, the ECJ should, in principle, observe the case law of the ECtHR,[9] however, a 'one-to-one' application of that case law is not always a possibility.

First of all, a comparison of the text of both articles reveals considerable differences, which raise the question of whether any link should be made whatsoever. A striking example of the difference between Article 17 Charter and Article 1 FP ECHR is that Article 17 Charter allows for the deprivation of the individual's possessions 'subject to fair compensation being paid in good time for their loss', while the article in the ECHR has no such criterion. Barkhuysen and Huijg note that 'both rights have an equivalent in the EU Fundamental Rights Charter, [...] which need not be discussed in more detail because it does not in principle have an added value in terms of the protection it provides in this regard'.[10]

However, Barkhuysen and Bos write that '[i]f the Charter contains a textual nuance that does not follow from the ECHR's case law, it cannot be ruled out that it must be interpreted as broader than the ECHR. See, for example, Article 17, which protects the right to property.'[11]

Although this observation by Barkhuysen and Bos is made specifically in respect of Article 17(2) of the Charter in connection with the additional subsection on intellectual property rights – which is absent from Article 1 FP ECHR – we do not rule out that, given the additional reference to fair compensation under Article 17(1) of the Charter as discussed above, the ECJ may find room, in certain situations, to substantiate an interpretation that would differ from the ECtHR's understanding of Article 1 FP ECHR.

9   This follows from Article 52(3) Charter (see below) and this is well-established case law of the CJEU.

10   T. Barkhuysen, T. Huijg, 'De omgang met bestaande pensioenrechten: het Europeesrechtelijke speelveld voor verplicht invaren en de methodiek van het zo nodig vrijwillig invaren', SDU, 2011 (our translation).

11   T. Barkhuysen, A.W. Bos, 'De betekenis van het Handvest van de Grondrechten van de Europese Unie voor het bestuursrecht' ['The significance of the Charter of the Fundamental Rights of the European Union for administrative law'], *JB-plus* 13.1 (2011). Whether their analysis refers to Article 17(2) or to Article 17(1) of the Charter is of little consequence; what matters is that a 'textual nuance' has been made.

5.2.2   ECJ case law

In addition to the above, it can be argued that the ECJ follows its own course
– in derogation from the case law of the ECtHR – and that the fundamental
property right will be given an interpretation and scope that differs from
the ECtHR's case law, namely a higher level of protection for individuals. The
first indication is case law of the ECJ. In these cases the ECJ tested against
Article 17 Charter without even referring to Article 1 FP ECHR.

A further indication that the Court of Justice will follow its own course is
found in the ground for exemption stated in Article 17 Charter. What should
the 'general interest' ground for exemption be taken to mean in the context of
the Charter, the ground for exemption that is also part of Article 1 FP ECHR?
The explanatory memorandum issued along with the Charter shows that
the general interest objectives acknowledged by the Union refer both to the
objects set out in Article 3 of the EU Treaty and the other interests that are
protected by specific provisions of the treaties, such as Article 36 TFEU (Treaty
of the Functioning of the European Union). Article 36 TFEU provides that:

> The provisions of Articles 34 and 35 shall not preclude prohibitions or
> restrictions on imports, exports or goods in transit justified on grounds of
> public morality, public policy or public security; the protection of health
> and life of humans, animals or plants; the protection of national treasures
> possessing artistic, historic or archaeological value; or the protection of
> industrial and commercial property. Such prohibitions or restrictions
> shall not, however, constitute a means of arbitrary discrimination or a
> disguised restriction on trade between Member States.

This means, amongst other things, that the Charter's fundamental rights
must be interpreted within the scope of the European Union's objectives,
including the economic free movement objective and the internal market,
as preserved in the TFEU.

In the *Schmidberger* case[12] the ECJ already set off the freedom of expres-
sion and freedom of assembly against the free movement of goods.[13] In the
more recent *Viking*[14] and *Laval*[15] cases, the ECJ assessed the collective action

---

12   Case C-112/00.

13   J. Morijn, 'Balancing Fundamental Rights and Common Market Freedoms in Union Law:
Schmidberger and *Omega* in the Light of the European Constitution', *European Law Journal* 12.1
(2006).

14   Case C-438/05.

15   Case C-341/05.

of trade union organizations against the freedom of establishment and services, respectively.[16] As Prechal and De Vries[17] have noted, an important merit of the judgements in *Viking* and *Laval* is that, for the first time, in relation to the internal market, the Court explicitly indicated that the EU not only has an economic purpose, but also a social one, which means that the rights resulting from the free movement provisions must be weighed against the aims of social policy, such as an improvement in living and working conditions and adequate social protection.[18]

It can be argued that (converting) pension rights also falls within this category. Although the judgements in *Viking* and *Laval* had many critics, who argued that the fashion in which the Court proceeds in the concrete balancing in these cases is not really convincing,[19] the ECJ, in later case law, persisted in trying to find the right balance between the internal market and the fundamental rights.

In addition to the above, it should be noted that the ECJ has already ruled that a Member State can be held liable under EU law if a pension fund entity does not meet certain liabilities towards the participant that should have been protected under proper implementation of relevant EU directive provisions. It follows from the *Hogan* case[20] that payment of 49% of pension benefit commitments by a pension fund entity is an absolute minimum threshold in this respect. If a pension fund entity's payments drop below this threshold, the Member State could in principle be liable if a breach of its EU law obligations can be substantiated.[21] In such a case, the private (second pillar matter) pension arrangement could be transformed into a state budget (public) matter. It is also worth pointing out the final sentence of Article 52(3) Charter, which provides that Charter rights corresponding to ECHR rights, must be applied in line with the manner in which the ECHR rights are guaranteed. Cleary, as was demonstrated above, these rights do not correspond, irrespective of what the explanatory memorandum to the Charter may suggest. What is more, this article does not prevent EU law from providing more extensive protection, also in connection with the relevant EU directives that are developed to ensure protection for EU citizens.

16   Case C-438/05.
17   S. Prechal, S.A. de Vries, '*Viking/Laval* en de grondslagen van het internemarktrecht', *Tijdschrift voor Europees en economisch recht* 11 (2008).
18   Idem.
19   P. Syrpis, T. Novitz, 'Economic and Social Rights in Conflict: Political and Judicial approaches to Their Reconciliation', *European Law Review* 33.3 (2008).
20   C-398/11.
21   Idem.

5.2.2.1   The Hogan *case[22]*

The facts of this case were the following. The claimants in the main proceedings against the Irish State were ten former employees of Waterford
Crystal, a manufacturer of crystal based in Waterford, Ireland, most of
whom had not yet reached their retirement age. For the claimants one of
the conditions of employment was that they would join one of the defined
benefit supplementary pension schemes set up by their employer (in EU
language: a supplementary system of social security benefits with awarded
benefits). In early 2009 a receiver was appointed for Waterford Crystal and
it was found to be insolvent. The supplementary pension schemes set up by
that company were wound up on 31 March 2009. According to their actuary,
the claimants would only receive between 18 and 28% of the actual value
of their accrued old age pension rights. The actuary retained by Ireland
found that this percentage was between 16 and 41%. In any case, neither
calculation approached the 49% referred to by the ECJ in the judgement
in *Robins and Others*.[23] The claimants in the main proceedings brought an
action against Ireland, claiming that Ireland had not properly transposed
Article 8 of Directive 2008/94. Ireland argued that it had adopted, both before
and after the judgement in *Robins and Others*, many measures designed
to protect the interests of beneficiaries of supplementary occupational
pension schemes. The Irish High Court decided to refer seven questions
to the ECJ for a preliminary ruling. In short, need there to be a causal link
between the claimants' loss of their pension benefits and the insolvency of
their employer for the directive to be applicable and is the Irish state liable
if it were established that Article 8 had not been transposed correctly? In
Hogan the ECJ provides an answer to these questions.

Directive 2008/94 of the European legislature of 22 October 2008 intends
to protect employees when their employer becomes insolvent. A key recital
of the directive is Recital 3, which reads:

> It is necessary to provide for the protection of employees in the event
> of the insolvency of their employer and to ensure a minimum degree of
> protection, in particular in order to guarantee payment of their outstand-
> ing claims, while taking account of the need for balanced economic and

---

22   Parts of this paragraph appeared in H. van Meerten, 'European Ruling on Pensions: Second
Warning for the Netherlands', in F.A.N.J Goudappel and E. M.H. Hirsch Ballin (eds), *Democracy
and Rule of Law in the European Union: Essays in Honour of Jaap W. de Zwaan* (The Hague: Asser
Press, 2016).

23   C-278/05.

social development in the Community. To this end, the Member States should establish a body which guarantees payment of the outstanding claims of the employees concerned.

Article 8 of the directive, on which the case before the ECJ turned, reads:

Member States shall ensure that the necessary measures are taken to protect the interests of employees and of persons having already left the employer's undertaking or business at the date of the onset of the employer's insolvency in respect of rights conferring on them immediate or prospective entitlement to old-age benefits, including survivors' benefits, under supplementary occupational or inter-occupational pension schemes outside the national statutory social security schemes.

In 1991, in the judgement in *Francovich and Others*, the ECJ recognized the principle of state liability for the loss and damage caused to individuals as a result of breaches of Community law that may be attributed to the state. According to the ECJ this principle is 'inherent in the system of the Treaty'.

Since then it is clear that this principle applies to all breaches of Community law of which the act or omission forms part, irrespective of the state body. A breach of Community law by a Member State will be attributed to a government body and result in the obligation to make good loss and damage caused to the individuals suffering injury if:

– The rule of law infringed should be intended to confer rights on individuals
– The breach should be sufficiently serious
– There is a direct causal link between the breach and the damage caused to the individuals

If these conditions are met, the failure to take measures to transpose a directive to attain the result prescribed by this directive within the period laid down for that purpose will as such constitute a serious breach of Community law and may give rise to a right of reparation for individuals suffering injury.[24]

The claimants in the *Hogan* case argued that Article 8 imposed an obligation of result, and the Advocate-General shared their view. The ECJ, however, did not. Although it did find, for the first time, that 49% of the pension benefits to which the claimants were entitled was a minimum level, it also

24 C-178/94.

ruled that the considerable discretion allowed to the Member States is an important criterion in determining whether attaining 49% of the pension benefits constituted a sufficiently serious breach of Community law.

The ECJ in *Hogan* stated:

> It is apparent from consideration of the first question that, on account of the general nature of the wording of Article 8 of the Directive, that provision allows the Member States considerable discretion for the purposes of determining the level of protection of entitlement to benefits.[25]

Directive 2008/94 must be interpreted as follows: the measures adopted by Ireland following the judgement of the Court of Justice of the European Union of 25 January 2007 in *Robins and Others* (C-278/05) do not fulfil the obligations imposed by that directive and the economic situation of the Member State concerned does not constitute an exceptional situation capable of justifying a lower level of protection of the interests of employees as regards their entitlement to old age benefits under a supplementary occupational pension scheme.

Directive 2008/94 must be interpreted as meaning that the fact that the measures taken by Ireland subsequent to *Robins and Others* have not brought about the result that the plaintiffs would receive in excess of 49% of the value of their accrued old age pension benefits under their occupational pension scheme is in itself a serious breach of that Member State's obligations.

In *Hogan*, the ECJ did find that Article 8 of the directive entailed an obligation of result. The mere fact that a minimum level of protection is not attained – in this case due to the employer's insolvency – leads to state liability.

This raises the interesting question of whether the obligation of 49% must also be performed without an insolvency of the employer, e.g. in the event of a de facto insolvency of the pension fund.

It is worth pointing out that the ECJ noted in its judgement in *Hogan* that Article 8 of the directive gives rise to a general obligation to protect the interests of employees. It would not be a huge stretch to place the pension fund, as the manager of deferred wages, within the scope of the directive. The judgement is also 'new' because the ECJ made it clear that the consequences of the financial crisis ought not to play a part in the financing of the pension system.

The judgement in *Hogan* could have considerable implications. In the case of an employer's insolvency, no causal link has to be established between the

25 C-398/11.

employer's insolvency and the loss of pension rights. A breach of an obligation of result suffices for state liability. And this is all the more cogent in view of the considerable criticism of Europe by (some parts of) the pension sector. It is 'forgotten' or simply not mentioned that 'EU involvement' is aimed at facilitating the protection of members of pension schemes: payment of 49% of the pension benefit commitments is an absolute minimum threshold. If a pension fund drops below this threshold, the Member State is automatically liable. Whether this development will lead to a formal 'European pension guarantee fund' – which can be argued already exist to some extent – is yet unclear.

5.2.2.2   The Hampshire case

The case of *Hogan* was followed by *Grenville Hampshire v The Board of the Pension Protection Fund*.[26] In this case, the ECJ held:

> Article 8 of Directive 2008/94/EC of the European Parliament and of the Council of 22 October 2008 on the protection of employees in the event of the insolvency of their employer must be interpreted as meaning that every individual employee must receive old-age benefits corresponding to at least 50% of the value of his accrued entitlement under a supplementary occupational pension scheme in the event of his employer's insolvency.

In circumstances such as those in the main proceedings, Article 8 of Directive 2008/94 has direct effect and may, therefore, be invoked before a national court by an individual employee in order to challenge a decision of a body such as the Board of the Pension Protection Fund.'

In other words, Directive 80/987/EEC requires Member States to ensure that every individual employee receives at least 50% of the value accrued entitlement to old age benefits in the event that his employer becomes insolvent.

This is a clarification of *Hogan*.

5.3   Direct horizontal effect: The ECHR v Charter

It seemed that the ECJ, in the *AMS* and the *Google* cases, allowed that, under certain circumstances, the Charter can have a direct horizontal effect, and might therefore be successfully invoked by an individual against, for

26   C-17/17.

example, a relevant pension fund involved with the conversion of pension rights before the ECJ and national courts. This was affirmed in the *Bauer* case. The Charter can be invoked in disputes between individuals, possibly leading to the setting aside of domestic norms like those at issue in the main proceedings.[27]

As a striking difference with the Charter, the fundamental rights of the ECHR would in principle not have direct (horizontal) effect in proceedings before the ECtHR effect since the ECHR can only be invoked against states. In the ECtHR case of *Tierfabriken* the Court held: 'The Court does not consider it desirable, let alone necessary, to elaborate a general theory concerning the extent to which the Convention guarantees should be extended to relations between private individuals *inter se*.'[28]

Furthermore, in all ECHR states, the ECHR needs to be transposed into national law; in the Netherlands via Articles 93 and 94 of the Dutch constitution. EU law does not, in principle, need that transposition. However, that does not mean that the ECHR fundamental rights, such as the property right, cannot have so-called *Drittwirkung*,[29] i.e. have (indirect) horizontal effect in national proceedings. However, that *Drittwirkung* of property rights depends on the transition mechanism of international law in national law. Therefore, the collaboration of a pension fund – in principle operated as an independent undertaking – with acts of government that facilitate conversion make the pension fund potentially liable under Article 17 of the Charter and potentially even (albeit indirectly) under the ECHR. However, given the different legal status of EU law as described above, the outcome of testing conversion against the Charter might differ from that under the ECHR.

There is a further difference in this respect between the ECHR and EU law. From the case law of the ECJ it can be inferred that, in principle, a wider range of parties might fall under the scope of the free movement articles of the TFEU, particularly where a general or public role of the relevant party can be identified.[30]

---

27   C-569/16 and C-570/16. See: http://eulawanalysis.blogspot.com/2018/11/you-can-teach-new-court-mangold-tricks.html.

28   ECtHR, *Tierfabriken v Switzerland* (2001), Application No. 24699/94, para. 46.

29   *Drittwirkung*, or the doctrine of the third-party effect, refers to the legal concept that an individual has the constitution right to sue another individual or the government. This is the term often used in Germany. See opinion of AG Cruz Villalón in Case C-447/09.

30   For example, the *Commission v France* (*Spanish Strawberries*) and *Schmidberger* cases (concerning private action by farmers and an environmental organization, respectively), which constituted the obstacle to free movement. In the *Viking* and *Laval* cases it concerned the

Against this background, it is not stretching the point too far to state that the test against the property rights in relation to a pension fund (a 'pure' (horizontal) direct effect) would probably work out differently from a test in relation to (a private act that is attributable to) an act of the government. And it seems that the results of a relationship governed by ECHR (public) law cannot 'simply' be transposed to a relationship that is (also) subject to the principles of direct horizontal effect under EU law. A thorough comparison between the Article 1 FP ECHR and Article 17 of the Charter, as to when an act of government is attributable to a Member State and/or when a pension fund is actually liable under both property articles, is warranted. In the sphere of pensions and employment, the development of a 'horizontal dimension' of fundamental rights and general principles is relatively recent.[31]

5.4 Application of the Charter to pension institutions

It cannot be ruled out that the Charter is applicable to the conversion of pension rights serviced by pension funds, provided that it can be substantiated that the operations of the pension fund are indeed within the scope of EU law provisions. If, in the case at hand, the free movement provisions could be invoked in relation to the IORP as a cross-border service provider, this would entail the application of the Charter. Consequently, in respect of cross-border pension arrangements provided by a IORP, a conversion of pension entitlements could directly fall within the scope of the Charter.

The IORP II Directive itself does not contain a direct provision on the conversion of pension rights and entitlements, however, the IORP II Directive does indirectly provide some general considerations which, it can be argued, have implications for the legal status of a conversion. Article 14(2) of the IORP II Directive states that a Member State may allow an institution – for a limited period of time – to operate with insufficient assets to cover the technical provisions that arise in connection with relevant pension entitlements. In such cases, the competent authorities shall require the institution to adopt a concrete and realizable recovery plan in order to ensure that the requirements of funding the technical

---

actions of trade unions. And we note that in a Dutch context, a pension fund has the statutory and legal obligations to serve in the best interest of the participants, and could in principle engage in resisting the immediate co-operation with conversion if the legal substantiation of the conversion would in the judgement of the pension fund be insufficiently provided for.
31 Opinion of AG Cruz Villalón, Case C-447/09.

provisions are met. Consequently, on the basis of the IORP Directive, the authorities are, under certain conditions, allowed to take a flexible approach in assessing the asset side of the balance sheet of the IORP. However, the IORP Directive does not seem to provide for flexibility in respect of the treatment of pension entitlements and the outstanding obligations of the IORP in connection with them. Given the fact that a conversion of pension entitlements serviced by an IORP needs to conform with IORP requirements, such a conversion could have implications under the IORP Directive. This would also imply that the Charter could in principle be invoked by relevant parties in such a case.

On the basis of the free competition provisions under the TFEU, a further observation could be made in respect of Dutch pension funds. The ECJ held in the case of, inter alia, *Albany* that a pension fund charged with the management of a supplementary pension scheme in the context of a collective agreement,[32] concluded between organizations representing employers and workers in a given sector (social partners), to which affiliation has been made compulsory by the public authorities for all workers in that sector, is an undertaking within the meaning of the EU Treaty.[33] Mandatory participation of employers and employees in a Dutch pension fund is a breach of the EU's free competition and free movement provisions, although it may be justified as long as the pension plan meets the – quite general – solidarity criteria of the ECJ. In relation to the legal position of pension participants and their mandatory participation in a Dutch pension fund entity, the protection of their pension rights falls under relevant EU law restrictions and consequently Charter rights also come into play.

The *Hogan*, *Viking* and *Laval* cases contain a further indication that (the servicing of) pension rights – established by the social partners in the context of collective bargaining agreements – could fall within the ambit of general EU law and thus, since it is primary EU Law, of the Charter. This clearly needs further consideration, but if, in a case at hand, general EU law provisions are applicable to Member States' actions, this should in practice imply that EU citizens would have access to the fundamental rights under the Charter.

---

32   The collective agreement fell outside the scope of Article 81 EC (now 101 TFEU).
33   Case C-67/96.

5.5 Conclusion

To conclude, it has been pointed out that the list of corresponding articles in the explanatory memorandum to the Charter is not entirely accurate, since 'that list also includes articles of the Charter 'whose meaning is wider', as well as articles of the Charter 'whose meaning and scope' are wider than those of the corresponding Articles of the ECHR'.[34] Therefore, it can be inferred from EU cases, most prominently *Bauer*,[35] that, if the Charter applies, individuals may directly rely on the Charter against the Netherlands (or against another Member State of the EU, vertically) and in some circumstances may even rely on it directly against another individual and/or the Dutch pension fund (horizontally) in national and ECJ proceedings if a breach of a fundamental right is at issue.[36] This might be the case if the provisions of the Charter alone meet the criterion of direct effect, and (if not), in connection with other secondary EU law, such as directives.

34 K. Lenaerts, 'Exploring the Limits of the Charter of Fundamental Rights', *European Constitutional Law Review* 8.3 (2012).

35 Ibid.

36 This is also in line with the opinion of the Centre of Expertise on European Law of the Dutch Ministry of Foreign Affairs: http://www.minbuza.nl/ecer/eu-essentieel/handvest-grondrechten.

6   PEPP

6.1   Introduction

On 29 June 2017, the European Commission proposed a framework for a pan-European personal pension product (PEPP).[1] This framework aimed to offer EU citizens a value-for-money option to acquire an income after retirement. Furthermore, the PEPP could help in meeting the objectives of the capital markets union (CMU), by increasing voluntary pension savings, aiding savers by expanding the available market of personal pension products and by enabling providers to offer products to a larger customer base.[2]

The PEPP is a one-of-a-kind initiative within the CMU package. While most European legislation governing pensions is aimed at establishing requirements for pension providers, the PEPP creates a 'label', guaranteeing the quality of certain features of the product itself. It may be argued that the PEPP is more of a retail finance product than a classic 'pension' product as such. If the PEPP turns out to be a success, more European labels for financial retail products may follow, such as mortgages or second pillar pension products.

Despite the freedom of services and capital, no pan-European personal pension product is readily available for consumers. One of the key features of the PEPP is that it is a portable product, in which savers can continue to contribute after moving from one Member State to another, thus preventing the obligation to purchase a new personal pension every time a consumer changes residence between Member States.

However, considering that only 3.7% of the working population of the EU is considered a mobile worker,[3] the added value of the PEPP may be especially prevalent in Member States without well-developed multi-pillar pension systems.[4]

1   Proposal for a Regulation of the European Parliament and the Council on a Pan-European Personal Pension Product (PEPP) COM/2017/0343.
2   Impact assessment – SWD(2017)243/942000.
3   Annual Report on Intra-EU Labour Mobility, May 2017.
4   PE-615.263_01_EN.

Therefore, the aim of the PEPP proposal is twofold:

- To provide mobile citizens with an easy-to-acquire portable pension
- To make available safe personal pension products that consumers trust, in markets where no products are available or trusted[5]

The PEPP will be a voluntary and supplementary pension product and is often qualified as a third pillar product.[6] This means that it will not or should not change the national pension systems, nor interfere with any existing systems, such as mandatory occupational systems, as exist in the Netherlands.[7] Furthermore, as was stressed by different stakeholders and the European Economic and Social Committee,[8] the PEPP should not diminish the relevance of setting up a strong first and second pillar in the Member States.[9]

At the time of writing, the European Council has still to formally approve the outcome of the interinstitutional 'trilogue' negotiations before the PEPP can be formally adopted.

6.2   The pan-European personal pension product (PEPP)

6.2.1   Legal basis

The PEPP is first of all, by definition, a personal pension product. As was discussed in Chapter 2 of this book, the European Union does not have competences to determine pension systems of Member States.[10] However, by using the powers to enhance the internal market, the creation of a stand-alone regime (or framework) for a portable personal pension product falls under the scope of Article 114 TFEU and enables the Commission to put forward legislative proposals to stimulate the internal market and long-term savings within and throughout the Union.

---

5   A loss of trust is especially prevalent in Member States where certain pension funds are nationalized or where the government is planning to do so in the near future.

6   H. van Meerten, J.J. van Zanden, Pensions and the PEPP: The Necessity of an EU Approach, European Company Law Journal 15, no. 3. (2018); L. van der Vaart, H. van Meerten, 'De pensioen opPEPPer?', *Tijdschrift voor Pensioenvraagstukken* 22 (2017)

7   Fiche 3: Verordening Pan-Europees Persoonlijk Pensioenproduct (PEPP), 1-9-2017.

8   ECO/440-EESC-2017-03297-00-00-ac-tra.

9   See also various recitals in both the general approach of the Council and the position of Parliament.

10   See also: ECO/440-EESC-2017-03297-00-00-ac-tra.

The PEPP regulation does not interfere with any existing national legislation concerning pensions, nor with any prudential requirements as stipulated in various other legal acts such as the Solvency II and the IORP II. The PEPP is based on a 'second regime',[11] which is based on the same legal acts and legal implications as regular initiatives, but exists in parallel with national legislation.[12]

Besides being a second-regime initiative, another key aspect of the PEPP is that it creates a framework for a product, instead of a prudential regime for providers. The framework for the product has to be sufficiently adaptable, since matters that are pension related, such as the retirement age or tax incentives,[13] fall outside of the scope of the regulation. To that extent, the use of a second-regime legislative act broadens the possibility for the European Commission to put forward initiatives, but also limits its contents. As will be discussed below, any articles governing out-payments will have direct consequences for the eligibility of tax incentives. If the PEPP is not eligible for tax incentives in one Member State, but does qualify for incentives in another, the PEPP may lose its Pan-European character altogether.

One option to circumvent this problem would be to establish a harmonized tax regime for the PEPP specifically, which may also be on an opt-in basis, as was proposed by Rapporteur Sophie in 't Veld in her draft report.[14]

6.2.1.1   The freedom to provide services and the compartment approach

In accordance with Article 14 of the PEPP Regulation, the PEPP will be subject to the provisions concerning the freedom of services and establishment. This materialized in the portability service: PEPP savers may keep contributing to a PEPP that was purchased in another Member State than the Member State of current residence. This means that a saver who worked in the Netherlands and contributed to a personal pension plan may keep saving for retirement, with the same provider and under the same conditions[15] when he or she moves to Germany. In this respect, the PEPP is one of the first initiatives under the freedom to provide services that is aimed at consumers, instead of companies. In the Commission's proposal, it was

---

11   Or 29th regime.

12   See also the draft regulation on a common European sales law (CESL)

13   H. van Meerten, J.J. van Zanden, Pensions and the PEPP: The Necessity of an EU Approach, European Company Law Journal 15, no. 3. (2018)

14   Sophie in 't Veld, 'Draft Report: Tax Treatment of Pension Products, Including the Pan-European Personal Pension Product', PE 620.853v01-00.

15   However, local rules on accumulation have to be taken into account to ensure the eligibility with local tax law.

mandatory for providers to offer a PEPP in all Member States after the transitioning period of three years (Article 13(3) of the proposed regulation). However, both Parliament and Council disagreed with this approach, since it rendered the PEPP an excessively expensive product. In the end, at least two sub-accounts need to be available after the transition period of three years (Article 18 (3)).

A PEPP may consist of multiple compartments, or sub-accounts.[16] This means that after purchasing a PEPP in one country, an additional sub-account may be opened for another. This means that a change or residence may lead to a change in the corresponding investment rules, but not to the obligation for the PEPP saver to search for a new product, hence avoiding a variety of different income streams after retirement.

The compartment approach was taken as a way to circumvent the problems related to the 49 different tax regimes in the EU. In a study carried out by Ernst & Young, it is demonstrated that tax incentives are of crucial importance for the success of the PEPP and appears to be 'the main driver for consumer choice'.[17]

As is noted by the Parliament's rapporteur, In 't Veld, there seem to be 'two objectives that are diametrically opposed'.[18] On the one hand, PEPP needs to be attractive to consumers, and on the other hand, the file is limited by the tax constraints of 49 different regimes. Therefore, it appears that the national tax legislation may be the biggest hurdle for the success of the PEPP,[19] but also the one issue that cannot be addressed in the regulation itself.[20]

6.2.2   The PEPP as a framework

The PEPP regulation is first of all a PEPP framework; once a personal pension product matches all the criteria stipulated in the regulation and a provider has (1) requested the PEPP status and (2) the product has been authorized, that personal pension product is eligible to be sold as a PEPP. Only after authorization would the rules of the PEPP framework apply. As stated before, the landscape throughout the Union is varied. Therefore, when describing the PEPP as the product itself, the correct terminology would be 'a' PEPP. A

---

16   In the original proposal and the position of Parliament 'compartment' was used. Compartment and sub-account have the same meaning in this Chapter.

17   Ernst & Young, *Study on the Feasibility of a European Personal Pension Framework*, European Union, June 2017, FISMA/2015/146(02)/D.

18   PE615.263v01-00.

19   J.J. van Zanden, 'Het PEPP: is er nog een pijler op te trekken?', PensioenMagazine 34 (2017).

20   PE615.263v01-00.

multitude of PEPPs may exist, all with different product features that are tailored to the specific wishes of the consumer and the possibilities in the Member States. However, to ensure consumer protection all PEPPs must meet a set of harmonized requirements.

These harmonized requirements consist mostly of information requirements, rules on portability and complaint procedures for the consumers and limits on investment policies for the providers.

Before examining these harmonized requirements further, it is important to explore the definition of a PEPP according to the regulation.

Article 2(1) of the Commission proposal defines a personal pension product as

> a contract between an individual and an entity on a voluntary basis, with an explicit retirement objective and which provides for capital accumulation with only limited possibilities for early withdrawal and which provides an income on retirement.

A pan-European personal pension product is defined in Article 2(2):

> [A] long-term savings personal pension product, which is provided under an agreed PEPP scheme by a regulated financial undertaking authorised under Union law to manage collective or individual investments or savings, and subscribed to voluntarily by an individual PEPP saver in view of retirement, with no or strictly limited redeemability.

According to the definition of the Commission, the PEPP is firstly a long-term savings product. However, it may be argued that a PEPP is not by definition a savings product in *strictu sensu*, but rather an investment product with a long term investment horizon.This is reflected in the possibility for asset managers to offer the PEPP. Investment products may have the same limited redeemability options as saving products. As a remark, it must be noted that there is a lack of a clear definition or consensus of the elements of a 'pension product' on a European level besides the definition given in this regulation.

Both the European Parliament and the Council subscribe more or less to this definition, with the exception that the Parliament adds that the product must be complementary while the Council adds that it may not be a 'second pillar product'.[21] Both of these additions may prove redundant, since it is up to Member States to decide if a certain pension product is a second

---

21   According to the general approach of the Council and the European Parliament's position.

or third pillar product, and the addition of complementary is sufficiently broad to allow for employer-sponsored 'third' pillar products. In the end, both additions were added to the definition in Article 2 (1).

In the Regulation,[22] PEPPs may also be acquired by a representative of a group of PEPP savers, such as an independent savers association, creating the possibility for interest groups to purchase PEPPs fit for their members (Article 2 (2)). In cases like these, it is hard to maintain a strict legal division of pension pillars, such as envisioned by the Council in their position. Furthermore, it might be argued that the legal division of three pension pillars may not be suitable at all in cross-border cases.[23]

The pension framework allows a variety of providers to offer the PEPP, however, a provider must be regulated under EU law according to Article 6(1) of the PEPP regulation.

In conclusion, the PEPP framework must have enough flexibility to tailor to the specific needs of PEPP savers in different Member States, whilst maintaining a high level of consumer protection in all Member States.

6.2.3   The authorization of a PEPP

One of the most intensely debated topics of the regulation was the way a PEPP is authorized. The legislative proposal came in tandem with the revision of the ESAs,[24] complicating the debate on the powers of EIOPA.

According to the Commission's proposal, a PEPP may only be manufactured and distributed after it has been authorized by EIOPA (Article 4). Once a PEPP has been authorized, the label will be valid in all Member States, allowing providers to benefit from markets of scale. As a preliminary

---

22   Report on the Proposal for a Regulation of the European Parliament and of the Council on a Pan-European Personal Pension Product (PEPP) (COM(2017) 343).

23   H. van Meerten, J.J. van Zanden, Pensions and the PEPP: The Necessity of an EU Approach, European Company Law Journal 15, no. 3. (2018)

24   The ESA's review aims to strengthen the mandates, governance and funding of the ESA's: Proposal for a Regulation of the European Parliament and of the Council Amending Regulation (EU) No 1093/2010 establishing a European Supervisory Authority (European Banking Authority); Regulation (EU) No 1094/2010 establishing a European Supervisory Authority (European Insurance and Occupational Pensions Authority); Regulation (EU) No 1095/2010 establishing a European Supervisory Authority (European Securities and Markets Authority); Regulation (EU) No 345/2013 on European venture capital funds; Regulation (EU) No 346/2013 on European social entrepreneurship funds; Regulation (EU) No 600/2014 on markets in financial instruments; Regulation (EU) 2015/760 on European long-term investment funds; Regulation (EU) 2016/1011 on indices used as benchmarks in financial instruments and financial contracts or to measure the performance of investment funds; and Regulation (EU) 2017/1129 on the prospectus to be published when securities are offered to the public or admitted to trading on a regulated market.

remark, it must be noted that those markets of scale are subject to different cultural preferences, which means that the likelihood that a PEPP can be successfully sold throughout the entire Single Market remains small. Rather, providers may aim to identify regions with similar pension cultures[25] or with a high degree of worker mobility.[26]

While Parliament supported the Commission approach for an important role for EIOPA, the Council deemed an increased role for EIOPA undesirable. National supervisory authorities were deemed to be 'closer' to the markets and more suitable to safeguard consumer interests. EIOPA should act as a register, should focus mainly on coordination and cooperation between national competent authorities and should therefore not exceed its existing competences.[27]

This opinion was reflected in the Council's general approach, which removed most of EIOPA's competences concerning the PEPP altogether. As stated before, negotiations on this topic were increasingly difficult, since they ran in parallel with the ESA's review. Member States are reluctant to transfer power to European authorities, fearing that such an approach would set a precedent for further transferral of powers to a European level.[28] On the other hand, having national supervisors authorizing a European product may lead to inconsistent quality between PEPPs that would disadvantage both saver and provider. Savers might not have access to adequately authorized products, while providers might suffer from the bias against some supervisory bodies.

In the final legislative text, EIOPA was granted product intervention powers similar to those in the PRIIPs (packaged retail and insurance-based investment products) regulation. With these powers, EIOPA can monitor the market for PEPPs and restrict or prohibit market access of certain PEPPs if they prove to be a significant threat to PEPP savers protection. A delegated act will be implemented to clarify such actions and the conditions in which they can be used.

The supervisory process is one of the key elements of the PEPP regulation, ensuring the same European product throughout all Member States. Regardless of the division of competences between the EU supervisory bodies and the national competent authorities, the author is of the opinion that a solid supervisory regime is of paramount importance for the PEPP.

25 For example, lump sum-based or annuity-based out-payments.
26 Such as the Dutch/German border.
27 See also Verslag van een schriftelijk overleg over het verzoek van de commissie om de ambtelijke instructies voor de raadswerkgroep ten aanzien van het voorstel voor de verordening pan-Europees Persoonlijk Pensioenproduct (PEPP-verordening), 5 September 2018.
28 Idem.

6.2.4   Eligible providers

Besides the supervisory and authorization process, the other political bot-
tleneck concerned the eligible providers of a PEPP. In the Commission's
proposal (Article 5), a variety of financial institutions are allowed to offer
the PEPP. These include:

- Credit institutions[29]
- Insurance undertakings[30]
- IORPs[31]
- Investment firms[32]
- Investment companies or management companies[33]
- Alternative investment funds[34]

All eligible providers are regulated under EU law, theoretically ensuring
an adequately level playing field. However, it must be noted that to some
degree the institutions fall under minimum harmonization regimes so that
some differences between Member States remain intact.

This minimum harmonization, especially concerning IORPs, lead to
debate in both the Parliament and the Council. Member States with mandatory enrolment systems and a high concentration of IORPs, such as the
Netherlands, Ireland and the UK, opposed the inclusion of IORPs, fearing
an interference in their national pension systems. In the Netherlands, it
was argued that the strict separation of the market between insurers and

29 Directive 2013/36/EU of the European Parliament and of the Council of 26 June 2013 on access
to the activity of credit institutions and the prudential supervision of credit institutions and
investment firms, amending Directive 2002/87/EC and repealing Directives 2006/48/EC and
2006/49/EC.

30 Directive 2009/138/EC of the European Parliament and of the Council of 25 November 2009
on the taking-up and pursuit of the business of Insurance and Reinsurance (Solvency II).

31 Directive 2016/2341/EU of the European Parliament and of the Council of 14 December 2016
on the activities and supervision of institutions for occupational retirement provision (IORPs)
(recast).

32 Directive 2014/65/EU of the European Parliament and of the Council of 15 May 2014 on
markets in financial instruments and amending Directive 2002/92/EC and Directive 2011/61/
EU.

33 Directive 2009/65/EC of the European Parliament and of the Council of 13 July 2009 on the
coordination of laws, regulations and administrative provisions relating to undertakings for
collective investment in transferable securities (UCITS) (recast).

34 Directive 2011/61/EU of the European Parliament and of the Council of 8 June 2011 on
Alternative Investment Fund Managers and amending Directives 2003/41/EC and 2009/65/EC
and Regulations (EC) No 1060/2009 and (EU) No 1095/2010.

pension funds would be weakened, overstepping the original mandate and legal basis for the PEPP regulation.[35]

Secondly, Dutch pension funds expressed concern about the possible implications of mandatory enrolment, especially because the case law that excludes social institutions such as pension funds from European competition rules explicitly mentions social character as one of the reasons for exclusion. Allowing social institutions to offer commercial third pillar products was deemed a risk. To counter these arguments, Parliament proposed to exclude IORPs that cannot cover biometric risks themselves and do not guarantee an investment performance or a certain level of retirement benefits. Furthermore, the liabilities from the PEPP should be ring-fenced. The Council took a similar approach, while in addition to having ring-fencing, added a Member State option, that was adopted in the final legislative text. IORPs eligible under national law to provide personal pensions shall be allowed to offer the PEPP as well.

While a Member State option by definition tailors to the national situations, it may also have some adverse effects on the internal market (for example, when an IORP from a Member State that allows for the provision of personal pension products wants to market in a Member State that doesn't). Consequently, providers may use 'partnerships' to open compartments in Member States in which the provider itself is not present. From the perspective of legal certainty, a Member State option approach is not optimal.

6.2.5   Distribution and information requirements

PEPP providers are by definition regulated under EU law. However, not all providers are subject to the same distribution regimes. Originally, the Commission proposed to have three categories of PEPP providers: providers under MiFID II,[36] under IDD[37] and a rest category that would have to comply with specific rules, as mentioned in Article 19 under c of the PEPP regulation.

One of the concerns of using the existing MiFID II and IDD regimes was that investment/insurance products are not necessarily well suited for retirement products. Because of this, Parliament decided to go for a

---

35 See the Dutch *pensioenfederatie*: E. Ablas, 'Het Pan-European Personal Pension Product: een wolf in schaapskleren?', *PensioenMagazine* 149 (2017).

36 Directive 2014/65/EU of the European Parliament and of the Council of 15 May 2014 on markets in financial instruments and amending Directive 2002/92/EC and Directive 2011/61/EU Text with EEA relevance.

37 Directive (EU) 2016/97 of the European Parliament and of the Council of 20 January 2016 on insurance distribution (recast), text with EEA relevance.

stand-alone regime, ensuring a level playing field between the different providers. However, adopting a third stand-alone regime next to the existing legislation (that was only recently implemented) and its accompanying delegated acts would prove to be an extra burden for providers, bringing along additional compliance costs which could potentially harm the uptake of the PEPP. For this reason, IDD and MifID II approach was adopted.

To try and ensure consumer protection and to prevent excessively costly products in the market, the consumer will be provided with multiple information documents, including a pre-purchase key information document (KID) and an annual PEPP benefit statement. The PEPP KID was based on the key information document in the PRIIPs regulation,[38] while the benefit statement has its origins in the IORP Directive.

Both the KID and the benefit statement are tailored to the specific needs of an individual pension saver, which meant that certain aspects needed to be removed while some other aspects were added in.[39]

Furthermore, both co-legislators decided against having execution only type of sales, emphasizing the long-term character of the product, as well as the limited redeemability, for which execution only was not a suitable instrument.

As will be explained in the next paragraph, a PEPP may have two investment strategies for its default option: a life cycle-based investment strategy or an investment strategy based on a capital guarantee. As capital guarantee based products are traditionally seen as the safer investment option, the inclusion of both life-cycling and a capital guarantee based Basic PEPP lead to having mandatory advice. While prospective PEPP savers will be well informed, having a (costly) mandatory advice might hamper the uptake of the PEPP.

6.2.6   The default and alternative investment options

In the Commission's proposal, providers are obliged to offer at least a default option and up to five alternative investment options. The default investment option (Article 37) shall ensure capital protection, based on a risk-mitigation technique that results in a safe investment strategy. The capital protection

---

38   Regulation (EU) No 1286/2014 of the European Parliament and of the Council of 26 November 2014 on key information documents for packaged retail and insurance-based investment products (PRIIPs).
39   For example, the IORP benefit statement is based on a collective pension scheme, which includes information on funding. These information requirements are not applicable on an individual product.

shall allow the PEPP saver to recoup the capital invested (Article 37(2) of the proposed regulation).

Especially in the beginning of the legislative process, a lot of attention was given to the definition of 'capital protection'. Insurers interpreted the word 'protection' as a capital guarantee, which would effectively rule out asset managers from offering the PEPP default option due to the applicable prudential requirements. However, a broader interpretation was given by asset managers, which argued that certain more conservative investment strategies known as 'life cycle' strategies would have the same result, but with the chance of higher returns.[40]

In the spirit of the regulation, the co-legislators decided to broadly interpret 'capital protection', allowing both capital guarantees and life cycling products as the default investment option.

The debate on what would be the preferred applicable investment option for a pensions product was mainly determined by the interpretation of the word 'pension'. Notwithstanding the individual and 'third' pillar character of the PEPP as a commercial product, some political groups deemed investment options without the provision of a guaranteed result too risky as a default option. For other political groups, the fact that (1) the consumer should be able to choose and (2) the life cycle investment option would have the chance of a higher return on investment was a reason to prefer the life cycle instead.

In the end, in both the European Parliament's position and the general approach by the Council, both options were inserted as a possible default option.[41]

Besides the mandatory default option, PEPP providers are allowed to offer six alternative investment option, as opposed to the original five in the Commissions proposal.

To avoid being locked in, PEPP savers are granted the right to switch every five years after conclusion of the PEPP contract.

To protect PEPP savers from cases like in the Netherlands were unreasonable costs were being charged in usurious insurance policies, so-called *woekerpolissen*, the co-legislatorsinstalled a 1% fee cap per annum for the default investment option. Stakeholders criticized this approach since the costs and fees would be higher for a capital guarantee than for other risk-mitigation techniques usually provided by asset managers, while consumer

---

40   C. Tebaldi, 'Consumer Protection and the Design of the Default Option of a Pan-European Personal Pension Product', Bocconi School of Management (2018).

41   Article 37 of both the general approach and the Parliament's position.

organizations welcomed the fee cap instead.[42] To tailor to the specific terms and conditions of different investment options, the definition of cost and fees will be further elaborated upon in second level legislation.

6.2.7   Investment rules

To qualify as a PEPP, the underlying investment strategy needs to be in line with the PEPP regulation. Like other legislative acts, such as the IORP II,[43] a role for ESG factors is foreseen. In Article 33 of the European Parliament's position, it is stipulated that providers are obliged to invest in such a way that the investment strategy mitigates risks concerning ESG factors and takes into account the long-term effects of said investments.

ESG factors are environmental, social and governance factors to determine the sustainability of investments. These factors co-exist next to the financial factors like profit. At the time of writing, no clear definition exist of what these factors entail, but it is expected that the European Commission will put forward acts to further clarify these factors, partly to prevent 'greenwashing' of investment strategies. At the time of writing, a proposal to define the environmental factors is being debated upon in both Parliament and Council.[44]

Because of these upcoming initiatives, no definition of ESG factors was put forward by the Commission. Parliament decided to define ESG factors as follows:

'[E]nvironmental, social and governance (ESG) factors' means the Union's climate and sustainability objectives as set out in the Paris agreement, the Sustainable Development Goals, the United Nations Guiding Principles on Business and Human Rights and the UNPRI definitions.

However, comments arose on the lack of a dynamic character of the definition, limiting the scope. For this reason, the following definition was adopted:

'[E]nvironmental, social and governance (ESG) factors' mean environmental, social and governance matters *such as* those referred to in the

---

42   BEUC, 'Trilogue Negotiations on European Commission's Legislative Proposal for a Pan-European Pension Product – BEUC Calls for a Cap on Costs', BEUC-X-2018-117, 10 December 2018, https://www.beuc.eu/publications/beuc-x-2018-117_proposal_for_a_pan-european_pension_product.pdf.
43   See Article 19 of the IORP II Directive.
44   Proposal for a Regulation of the European Parliament and of the Council on the establishment of a framework to facilitate sustainable investment, 2018/0178 (COD).

Paris Agreement, the Sustainable Development Goals, the United Nations
Principles on Business and Human Rights and the United Nations supported Principles of Responsible Investment definitions.

Sustainability and prudent investing play a big role in the financial sector,
in particular in the long-term strategies of pension providers. It is to be
expected that ESG factors will play an increasingly important role in the
near future.[45]

6.2.8   Out-payments

As stated before, the possible out-payments are relevant for the eligibility for
tax incentives in different Member States. For this reason, the Commission
chose not to harmonize any aspect in relation to the out-payment phase. If
the out-payments were to be harmonized, the PEPP would lose the possibility
for favourable tax treatment, which was considered one of the key factors
for the success of the regulation. This approach was shared by the Council
in their general approach.

Article 52 of the Commission's proposal mentioned four different out-
payment options.

– Annuities
– Lump sum
– Drawdown payments
– Combinations of the above forms

With these options, virtually all forms of out-payments are eligible for the
PEPP. This approach was shared by the Council in their general approach.
However, due to the long-term nature of the PEPP and the general principle
that pension products are to provide retirees with a replacement income,
the European Parliament chose to have additional harmonization of the
out-payment in the default option.

To prevent disturbing the level playing field, capital guarantee-based
investment options would have a maximum of 35% in lump sum out-payment
at the beginning of the decumulation phase, and 65% in annuities. Life-cycle
based Basic PEPPs would have their out-payments in a drawdown plan instead.

It could be argued that preferencing annuities of lump sum out-payments
is beneficial for the PEPP saver and prevents less financially educated savers

45   KPMG, 'Responsible Investing – A Fad or the Future?' (2018).

'from spending their money in Vegas',[46] but this argument has no scientific basis. In general, retirees are reluctant to spend their retirement savings and often underspend instead.[47] Furthermore, harmonizing the form of out-payments for the default PEPP may lead to less uptake in comparison with alternative investment options that do not have such limitations.

For these reasons, no harmonization of the decumulation phase was adopted. Instead, all conditions are left to Member State legislation. For the Basic PEPP, providers have to offer retirement planning to ensure the suitability of the chosen outpayment option for the individual PEPP saver. However, for alternative options such an obligation does not exist (Article 59).

6.3   Conclusion

As seen in the previous chapters, European legislation has had a major impact on national pension systems and institutions. The majority of these have had an effect on occupation pensions. With the PEPP, the European Union tries to create a framework, or hallmark, to ensure quality personal pensions for any citizen in the Union. To that extent, the PEPP initiative is one of the first capital market initiatives that target the individual consumer, instead of institutions. By regulating consumer protection, such as informational requirements and complaint procedures, the PEPP 'stamp' on a product will guarantee a properly supervised product that is safe and simple. The legislative act itself also shows the limitations of the competences of the Union. While the eligibility for tax incentives is the most important aspect of the success of the PEPP, it is also the sole subject the legislative act may not touch upon.

It is expected that the PEPP, once the legislative process finishes, will be a safe, simple and consumer-friendly product for mobile citizens, but even more for those who currently have no access to trusted retirement products in their own Member State of residence.

---

46   A commonly heard argument against the lump sum as an out-payment option.
47   FCA, Retirement Outcomes Review Interim Report, MS16/1.2 (2017).

Index

Albany 74
AOW *see* General Old Age Pensions act
Apf 90

BEPGs 36

Commission v Germany 72
Compulsory membership 66
   Belgium 85
   Denmark 82
   France 86
   Germany 83
   Netherlands, The 78
   Sweden 81
CSRs 36

Defined benefit 26, 117
Defined contribution 26, 117
Direct horizontal effect 136

EIOPA 34
EMU 34, 37
ESMA 34
EU competences 15, 28
European Semester 36

Freedom of movement 123
Freedom to provide services 66

Gebhard 72
General Old Age Pensions Act 25
General Pension Fund *see* Apf

Hampshire 136
Hogan 133

IIA *see* Interinstitutional Agreement on Better
   Law- Making
Impact Assessments 45
Interinstitutional Agreement on Better
   Law-Making 41, 45, 59
IORP 12, 16, 45
   Information requirements 120
   IORP Directive 21, 39, 91
   IORP II 100
   Supervision 120

Kattner Stahlbau 74

Occupational pensions 63
Open Method of Coordination 34
ORSA 48

PEPP 12, 17, 142
   Default and alternative investment
     options 151
   Distribution and information
     requirements 150
   Eligible providers 149
   Investment rules 153
   Out-payments 154
Property rights issue 128
Proportionality 43
Prudent Person Principle 109

Risk-Management Requirements 112

Säger 68
Services of General Economic Interest 70
Single Market Act 58
Subsidiarity 38

Three Pension Pillars 22
Tobacco Advertisement 31
Treaty on Stability, Coordination and
   Governance 36
Treaty on the European Union 22, 28
   Article 5(3) TEU 38
   Article 5(4) TEU 43
Treaty on the Functioning of the European
   Union 22, 28, 72, 102
   Article 106(2) 72
   Article 106(2) TFEU 70, 88
   Article 114 TFEU 30, 100, 143
   Article 148 TFEU 34
   Article 153 TFEU 100
   Article 289 TFEU 48
   Article 290 TFEU 50, 54, 102
   Article 291 TFEU 54
   Article 352 TFEU 33
   Article 36 TFEU 131
   Article 45 TFEU 27
   Article 52 TFEU 75, 88
   Article 56 TFEU 22, 66
Trias Politica 48

UNIS 77

Viking 72